NEW TECHNOLOGIES, NEW POLICIES?

A REPORT FOR THE BROADCASTING RESEARCH UNIT

JOHN HOWKINS

BFI Publishing

First published in 1982 by the British Film Institute
127 Charing Cross Road
London WC2H 0EA

British Library Cataloguing in Publication Data

Howkins, John

New technologies, new policies?
1. Communication – Technological innovation
I. Title
302.2'345   P96.T42

ISBN 0 85170 128 0

Printed by Tonbridge Printers Ltd, Tonbridge, Kent

Contents

Preface

This report covers the new technologies and services of communications broadcasting and video that are available or being planned in the UK at the beginning of 1982. It covers both technologies and services, and policies and legislation. It was written in March 1982. Some sections have been adapted from *InterMedia*, the journal of the International Institute of Communications.

Foreword

The Broadcasting Research Unit, which was set up just over a year ago, has three founding fathers: the BBC, the Markle Foundation (of the USA) and the BFI. The first two are providing funds, the third services in kind, such as accommodation.

The Unit's work is guided and overseen by a small Panel composed partly of representatives of the three establishing bodies, partly of others with specially relevant experience. The Panel and its unit are free agents; this independence and autonomy are crucial to it.

The Panel has several areas of interest such as, quite particularly, the implications of the new communications technologies (on which it has established a Working Party which will issue regular reports), the encouragement of joint enquiries linking broadcasters and external research workers, and the production of publications about issues on which urgent enquiries might be useful.

John Howkins' timely report, which is the first publication initiated by our Working Party, arises squarely from the BRU's first area of interest. It is not a statement by the Working Party. It is nevertheless a paper which both the Working Party (and the Panel) very strongly feel worth publishing.

Reading as a layman I found the report most helpful – dispassionate, level-headed, well-informed and very shrewd, a most compact and clear guide to the new technological jungle.

It is meant to lay the groundwork for better-nourished public discussion on the wider and – deeper – social decisions which now deserve urgently to be considered. John Howkins keeps his own judgments in the background but he points exactly to where judgments have to be made. Look in particular at Chapter 9, or consider only these two cogent passages:

> Most organisations analyse new technologies to see if they might challenge existing bureaucratic standards. Very few ask if new technologies can satisfy new social needs ... the hallmark of the information society is that policies on information and communication become a chief element in the national interest.

And, at a more detailed level:

It may well be that the easiest way forward for the new tv services would be to plunder the proven successes and attractions of the old.

The first battleground in that plundering operation, he reckons (and he is not alone), will be sport.

We are seeing in this decade a major threat to the very idea of public service broadcasting. That threat is partly explicit and direct, partly fortuitous and oblique. It comes from technological, commercial, economic and political interests. Some people could make a lot of money from a new free-for-all. Governments and some civil servants are so affected by the prospects for economic growth (employment, exports, etc.) which being first with the new technology promises that they are impatient of considerations which might slow up the drive to those rich pastures. True, we now have the Hunt Committee – of three! – on the wider issues; all honourable and distinguished men, no doubt. We will await their deliberations with the keenest interest.

Fifty years ago the structure of British broadcasting was established in a mood compounded of earnestness, the fear of anarchy on the air waves, a desire to ensure that 'sound' values predominated. It was both a conservative and a Conservative prescription. But the curious internal chemistry of society ensured that this regulatory framework became the climbing frame on which, and for all its faults, the best public service system in the world grew, one which sought to inform, educate and entertain, which tried to achieve balance and objectivity, which respected minorities of all kinds and which believed in the potentialities in all of us, our capacity to widen and deepen our interests. It would be a dreadful irony if, half a century later, a government strong in that other side of British Conservatism – intensely trade-, technology- and cash-conscious, proud of its aggressive competitiveness – were to send us into the Information Society with wholly inadequate social and cultural compass and rudder; without having thought adequately about how the best of the new may be married to the continuance and development of the best in the old; without redefining the public service idea for the late twentieth century.

RICHARD HOGGART
Chairman, BRU Panel

Introduction

During the course of its early deliberations the Working Party on New Technologies decided that it needed an accurate and comprehensive survey of developments in cable, video and satellite technology. In particular we wanted to know something of the state of technical developments and the kinds of decisions about those which either had been made or were in the process of being made. We asked John Howkins, widely regarded as one of the best informed journalists in Britain, to prepare such a report. He has done so, and with considerable skill has brought together a wide range of detailed information. We are pleased, therefore, that it is now being published and made available to a wider audience.

We welcome the report as a descriptive rather than prescriptive work. It is the first of what we hope will be a series of papers emerging from our activity as we move towards our own conclusions, which we anticipate reporting on in 1983. The issues we are trying to address will, we believe, affect the whole ecology of communications culture in this country well into the next century. Any decisions on the shape of that culture must be taken not from a position of wishful thinking, but from one of profound knowledge. We believe that John Howkins' *New Technologies, New Policies?* is an important first step towards that ideal.

ROBIN SCOTT
Chairman, Working Party on New Technologies

1 New Technologies, New Policies

1.1. In the old days the world of broadcasting and the world of film were self-contained, and for broadcasting the Home Office and for film the Department of Trade·were the exclusive sources of policy and regulation. Today, the technologies of information and communication can provide services as variegated as movie and hotel reservations, and the agents of policy range from the Home Office, to a special Cabinet unit on information technology, to British Telecom which is promoting something called 'picture Prestel'. The showcase for this new universe is not the trade shows of the broadcasting organisations and film companies but the discount stores in Tottenham Court Road selling home video.

1.2. But video and its blatant consumerism is only a sub-plot. The keynote is information technology (IT), which includes both information and communication, and not only technology but also systems, services and uses. The future of broadcasting and film, insofar as it involves new technologies, is part of the wider future of information technology. For this reason, if no other, the Cabinet Office's IT unit, which co-ordinates the Government's departmental IT activities, regards broadcasting as part of its domain; and few voices have proposed otherwise. Of course the Home Office will continue to maintain its responsibilities for the standards of British broadcasting; and the Department of Trade will continue to try to support the British film industry. But equally, policies on broadcasting and on film are becoming part of a wider discussion that includes considerations of industrial expansion (especially relevant to the decision about a British cable system), employment and consumerism.

1.3. The modern home has several means of electronic entry: telephone wires, the TV cable, the TV antenna. Each entry point shows marks of its origins and is owned and operated in unique fashion. The convergence of signals (e.g. videotex, electronic mail, subscription TV) is blurring the regulatory and cultural characteristics of each category. Not only are the devices complementary (e.g. cable, satellites) but also the services (e.g. news bulletins, teletext) and functions (e.g. multi-channel, time-shifting). Changes in one will often influence others. The sports results which used to be printed on paper and distributed by mechanical transport arrive by antenna and, for some, by telephone

1

wires and cables to be displayed on a TV screen. The greatest pressure for change comes from the imaginative use of cable and the encouragement of private competition in telecommunications (the chief issues now faced by the Cabinet Office's cable committees).

1.4. The USA provides a glimpse of the possible. In February 1982 as many as 23,726,220 households subscribed to cable, 29% of the total (Nielsen). Nine years ago pay-TV did not exist. Now it is a billion dollar industry with 12 million subscribers (Nielsen). Pay-TV is top of the agenda in the TV network companies, Wall Street and Hollywood. BBC programmes, once distributed on public television, are now reserved for a commercial pay-TV service.

1.5. Most people underestimate the amount of information technology they have. They will admit to a TV set, a radio set and perhaps a hi-fi. Yet the typical household actually has a TV set, several radio sets, a system for audio discs and a system for audio cassettes. Most people own a camera for taking still pictures, and a pocket calculator which, although they might be surprised to know it, contains several computer parts. Over two-thirds of the country's households are joined up to the telephone network; about one-third have a typewriter. Some people have two or even more TV sets, video cassette players, a film or video camera for moving pictures, video games and a home computer. About 2,500,000 households subscribe to a cable TV relay service, of which some 30,000 are expected to pay a premium subscription to receive a special pay-TV service of feature films.

1.6. Very few people are aware that many of these gadgets, sets, pieces of equipment are somehow related and that they can be increasingly linked together, either physically or in terms of the content. A Super-8 camera which takes pictures is related to a TV set which displays pictures. The potency of video is that each part of the system (the video camera, the video storer and the video display unit) is seen for what it is.

1.7. Many industries, hitherto very separate in their traditions, industrial practices and finances, are converging around this video nexus. The TV industry, the film industry, the music industry, telecommunications, publishing and computers, which at present operate under different government departments, regulations and conventions, are now finding themselves sub-industries of a whole new area of activity. The most obvious symptom of these changes is the development and marketing to the consumer of a range of new electronic technologies: video cassettes and discs, pay cable television, satellites, etc. But there is another more basic element, the national network that

2

has been created by the Post Office and British Telecom. The transition of the familiar telephone network into a complex, multi-level network providing many different services is absolutely central to the new information economy. British Telecom's development of its Integrated Switched Digital Network (ISDN), capable of providing everything from telephones to video, is the country's single most important industrial investment. Home video is private, the telecommunications network is public. Broadcasting stands betwixt these two elements, an amalgam of the public and the private, difficult to get right and now challenged by multiple new interpretations.

1.8. The trend towards more TV is not inevitable nor universally welcomed. West Germany, which for many years was a fervent supporter of new media technologies, shows the force of 'older' technologies and services. In 1976, the Bonn government set up a major commission into new telecommunications services (known as KtK after its German-language title). The KtK recommended that the government reject the proposals for a national broadband video network and give first priority to the narrowband network. Telephones and videotex, it suggested, were more important than cable television. Since then, the Bonn government has slightly changed its views. But the KtK's preference for the telephone over video is a salutary check on the enthusiasm for multi-channel television, and, of all European countries, West Germany is the most ambivalent about the benefits of information technology and broadband video.

1.9. According to a Thames *TV Eye* poll in March the British are also undecided. Asked if more TV channels would be a good idea or a bad idea, 64% said it was a good idea and 29% said it was a bad idea. Also, 35% believed more channels would damage the reputation of British television. Feature films were the most popular choice of material for the new channels, but only 32% said they were prepared to spend up to £10 a month to see recently released films.

1.10. This report surveys this muddled scene. It covers: (1) the UK's existing regulatory framework for broadcasting and other video services; (2) the new video technologies; and (3) government thinking and policy. But, compared to that tripartite scheme, neatly dividing technology and policy, it weaves a continuous strand between the woof of technology and the weft of regulation. It deals with 'old' and 'new' technology because sometimes it is impossible to make a sensible distinction as the focus shifts from a technology to a system, a service, a use, a market: is the UHF transmitter network of Channel Four old or new? The report is ordered in four parts, not according to the adversarial split of technology/regulation but rather according to the schema

3

of production, transmission, storage and display which has the powerful advantage that it applies to TV, to films shown in cinemas, and to publishing of all kinds.

1.11. The report is timely. The UK government, after years of neglect of information and communications matters, has just announced proposals 'in principle' for a national satellite broadcasting system and is also engaged in serious discussions about cable networks. This activity demonstrates the government's commitment to 'information technology' as the best bet for industrial renewal – and election success. A series of meetings that started in November under the auspices of Patrick Jenkin, Secretary of State for Industry, and Kenneth Baker, his Minister for Information Technology, led to a series of Cabinet decisions in late February. The satellite system was announced on 4 March 1982, followed by the publication of a Cabinet Office report on cable on 22 March. The UK is now in the forefront of European communications development.

2 Production

2.1. For many years the production of a good quality signal of video and sound was the dominant concern of researchers and engineers. Without a good originating picture good transmission and reception are almost irrelevant. Even today there is a major effort to produce better cameras; especially the cheaper, lightweight cameras that can operate in low levels of light. But the focus of research has moved: first to the means of recording, with the development of videotape in ever smaller formats and cheaper systems, and then to the means of home display and storage. This progression from production to reception, from industrial uses to the consumer, is typical of the electronics industry. It also increases consumer costs as a proportion of total costs. The viewers' costs of TV have always been more than the broadcasters' costs; the ratio is set to increase dramatically.

2.2. The UK production industry consists of several sectors that tend to operate quite separately; feature films financed by British money and made in Britain; foreign feature films that have a UK component for technical or fiscal reasons; commercials; industrial, educational, etc. films; and films made for television. Some sectors are buoyant; some are depressed. British features have not done well for many years, but the Oscar-winning success of *Chariots of Fire,* and the mostly domestic achievement of *Gregory's Girl* and other features have made the industry more optimistic than for many years.

2.3. The industry may have to reform many of its current practices, including its financial practices, if it is to take advantage of the new opportunities. The trigger for change is Channel Four, which is now commissioning at an annual rate of about £100 million. Another factor is the promise of multiple outlets via cable, satellites, cassette, disc, etc. which raise the chances of increased revenue over many years; the equivalent of a book publisher's valuable 'back list'. These new outlets will affect the ways in which the broadcasting organisations and other distributors finance the making of programmes; both the amount paid and the rights bought. The money for new production must come from the organisations that can raise income from the audience; other sources of money can only be limited or temporary. Part of this restructuring of the film industry will be changes in the traditional pattern of release. Producers may maximise income by exploiting a hierarchy of release, perhaps selling first to pay-TV before selling to disc, cassette and 'free' TV. Cinema exhibition may take place at an early stage (to maximise press publicity) or later. The need for flexibility in release schedules may require some change in the current restrictions on the showing of films on television until they are three years old and on cable until they are one year old. The BBC has already said that it hopes to broadcast feature films on its satellite pay-TV service before they are shown in cinemas.

2.4. The costs continue to rise. Film on location is increasing the most, with video in the studio becoming relatively more attractive. One example may suffice: the producer of a BBC drama series with 12 episodes planned for 1982/83 calculated it would cost £40,000 per episode more to shoot film at Ealing (in the cheapest manner possible) than to record on tape at Television Centre. The whole series of 12 episodes would have cost £500,000 more on film than on video. These production costs can be related to programme prices. What is the cost per hour to make; and to buy? Given a fixed revenue (from advertising or licence) will satellites or cable be cheaper and thus leave more money for programme purchases? So far, economic analyses of the new media look only at costs to the users. But we should also look at the amounts of money available for production.

2.5. There has emerged recently a whole new field of activity: home production. Home video cameras for moving pictures are becoming much cheaper. It is possible to buy a decent colour video camera for about £600. This price will come down. Moreover, in a world notorious for incompatible equipment it is surprising and heartening to see that five major manufacturers (Matsushita, Hitachi, Sony, JVC and Philips) are close to signing an agreement on a new 8mm standard format for both cameras and cassettes, which would affect both availability and costs. This new 8mm video standard is not intended to replace the half-inch (12mm) format now used by VHS, Betamax and Philips V2000, but it could provide a model for the next generation.

2.6. Video still photography is also challenging the existing conventions. The Sony Mavica (magnetic video camera) records electronically on a magnetic disc, and so can store pictures very easily and display them immediately. The full system includes devices to show the pictures on a TV set, print them on paper, and transmit them down a telephone line. The Mavica camera to be launched in Japan in late 1983 at around £350 is designed to compete with the professional 35mm market, and a cheaper consumer version may be some years away. The quality of picture registration and display will probably have to be improved before any consumer launch. Sony's commitment

6

to 'Mavigraphy' is very substantial, but Kodak, which has invested heavily in video research, is countering not with its own video camera but with a completely new electronic disc camera that uses a magnetic cartridge. The Kodak Disc 4000–8000 range shows a loyalty to film, not a switch to video.

2.7. The future of video cameras, for both moving and still images, is ineluctably bound up with the future of the TV set as the video display unit and probably with cassette storage systems as well. The linkage is a good illustration of the interdependence of all video, which runs like a motif through this report.

3 Distribution: Broadcasting by Terrestrial Transmitters

3.1.1. By far the greatest advances have been made in the fields of distribution and transmission – in other words, not information technology but communications technology, although the prevailing wisdom makes no differentiation. This chapter and the two that follow cover wireless broadcasting by terrestrial transmitters; wireless broadcasting by satellite transmitters; and distribution by wires and cables. There are other means of distribution. Retail outlets and mail order are increasingly significant in many video sectors, not only in entertainment but also in instruction and in purchasing. It is not surprising that such diverse organisations as American Express, the Open University, W. H. Smith and Sears Roebuck were among the first explorers of video.

3.1.2. The use of the electromagnetic spectrum and radio waves to distribute sound and moving images over large areas of land, without wires and instantaneously, is one of the great and most perplexing achievements of modern times. The very earliest experiments in wireless telegraphy (1895), sound broadcasting (the 1920s) and television broadcasting (the 1930s) were supported by private entrepreneurs; but in each case the state soon established a public monopoly on both technical and political grounds. In the UK it was many years before the monopoly was fractured; and, indeed, monopolistic conditions have remained in broadcasting after the establishment of private television in 1955 and private radio in 1973; and, in telecommunications, after the passing of the 1981 British Telecommunication Act which allowed private companies to compete with British Telecom, both in equipment (e.g. PABXs, telephones) and in services (e.g. the Mercury high-speed network).

3.1.3. The starting point for the regulation of broadcasting is the 1949 Wireless Telegraphy Act (sections 1 and 2) which gives the Home Office wide powers to regulate the use of the frequency spectrum. The Home Office has two departments concerned with these matters: the Radio Regulatory Department, and the Broadcasting Department. It is not insignificant that they live some distance apart; the RR Department in Waterloo Bridge House and the Broadcasting Department in Queen Anne's Gate. The Radio Regulatory Department is responsible for all UK uses of the frequency spectrum. These uses include the fixed services (e.g. point-to-point telecommunication services like telephony), mobile services (e.g. car radios), radionavigation, radio astronomy, etc.; of the total, broadcasting is only a small part. The Broadcasting Department is responsible for the more specific matter of the licensed broadcasting organisations.

3.1.4. The context of radio regulation is set by agreements reached in the International Telecommunication Union (ITU), the UN agency based in Geneva which is responsible for the international management of several key telecommunications issues (mainly standardisation and co-ordination), and which has an increasingly important influence on British national policy.

3.1.5. The ITU does a great deal of its work at World or Regional Administrative Radio Conferences (WARCs or RARCs) which fix service conditions and allocate groups (bands of contiguous) frequencies to a service. It also holds conferences on frequencies that have been already allocated to services, to assign them to specific countries. For instance in 1971 it held a WARC to allocate several bands of frequencies to the broadcasting satellite service; a few years later, in 1977, it held another conference to assign those bands to individual countries.

3.1.6. The Home Office has total control over the licensed use of all frequencies. A frequency may be allocated to a service or even specifically assigned to the UK for many years before the Home Office will allow it to be used. The saga of Channel Four, the country's fourth UHF television channel, which was allocated decades ago but not licensed to the IBA until 1980, is an obvious example. Indeed the Home Office has an established reputation for being reticent, even secretive, about the UK's available spectrum resources.

3.1.7. Arguments over the possible number of local radio stations started long before the debate on Channel Four; and still continue. And the proclaimed 'technical facts' about other services, notably mobile radio (in 1978) and Citizens' Band (in 1980/1), have proved equally contentious. Yet there is sometimes a need for quick action. A great deal of the frustration over CB might have been avoided if the Home Office had acted more quickly.

3.1.8. The issue raised by these new techniques is the central one of licensing. At the moment the Home Office must devise and implement a licensing system for each kind of use: whether it be a national broadcasting service, pay-TV or Citizens' Band. It must decide, before each service starts, what each service shall be. It has to set the conditions of the licence, set a licence fee and then monitor (or not) the licensed use. For this task it has few guidelines. For all new services it will be receiving advice from a mix of partisan interests, mostly from commercial companies that wish to manufacture or sell the new equipment and from those who wish to use it. Licensing – especially of commercial use – is the key issue for the next five years. But both the concept and the practice are often misunderstood.

3.1.9. The Home Office has licensed two public authorities to provide broadcasting services: the British Broadcasting Corporation (1927), and the Independent Television Authority (1955), which later became the Independent Broadcasting Authority (1971). The BBC started sound broadcasting in the 1920s and the first full national TV service in the 1940s. The ITA started ITV in 1955. Ten years later the BBC opened BBC-2. A longer interval was to pass, and not without controversy, before the IBA was given, under the 1980 Broadcasting Act, the opportunity to operate 'a second television service'.

THE BBC

3.2.1. The BBC's Royal Charter and the BBC Licence and Agreement, the instruments which constitute the British Broadcasting Corporation, were renewed in 1981 for 15 years ending in 1996. The Charter and licence are often referred to as guaranteeing the BBC's freedom. But both documents are also concerned with restrictions. They do not say the BBC shall be independent without restrictions; they say it must provide certain services in a certain manner and that, if the BBC fulfils its obligations the government will not intervene.

3.2.2. The new Charter contains several innovations. The BBC's basic objective remains the broadcasting of public services to the general public. But cable services are acknowledged and permitted and satellites are included. Article 3(b) says that, subject to the [Home] Secretary of State's prior approval the BBC may provide, 'as public services, by means of wireless telegraphy, other services'. In other words the BBC may provide narrowcasting as well as broadcasting; it may even provide specialised text and data services. Article 3(h) says that the BBC, again subject to Home Office approval, may 'construct or acquire . . . stations in space' (i.e. satellites), and use them for broadcasting; interestingly the article specifically mentions broadcasting to 'countries' in the plural. As for constructing, acquiring or using a non-UK satellite the text is ambiguous. The corporation may not acquire any licence or concession (Article 4) from a foreign government without the prior approval of the Secretary of State; and the wording of the article is not encouraging. But what about a licence or concession granted by a private company?

3.2.3. The Charter and Licence set the BBC's framework, and thus financial framework, for all its activities. The financial rules are restrictive. The Treasury minutes (2 April 1981) prefacing the Licence emphasise that money provided for the Home Services (i.e. everything except the External Services) may not, without the Secretary of State's approval, be used for the purposes of a subscription broadcasting service. Sponsored programmes (section 12) and advertising are ruled out. It is worth noting, however, that the Director General designate is not so opposed to advertising as his predecessors have been. In the past, the BBC did not sell airtime on grounds of principle. It was felt very strongly by all staff that both in general terms and on specific occasions the presence of advertisements would damage the independent reputation of the BBC. But Alasdair Milne, when Managing Director, BBC-TV, has given quite different factors as his reasons: 'We have established to our own satisfaction that there simply isn't enough advertising in this country to support the BBC (which in the current financial year will spend £535 million) and ITV and the Fourth Channel and breakfast television and the local press and so on. We've been knocked about a bit for being too "ideological" about this – maybe rightly – which is why we believe that the distinction between the public service broadcasting system and the commercial system is now quite clear and established. Advantages accrue to both, and if we had a totally commercial system in this country all the evidence from around the world is that broadcasting as a whole would suffer' (*Radio Times,* September 1981). In this view, the main reason is pragmatic (would it work?) and even the moral argument has been downgraded from one of high principle to the more pejorative term of 'ideology'. Since then, moreover, the 'clear and established' distinction between the BBC and the commercial system has rapidly become blurred. The mixing of BBC and ITV programmes, and advertisements, on the Welsh Fourth Channel may be a special case. But it is difficult to discern distinctions of motive and practice as the BBC moves first into pay-TV and satellites.

3.2.4. For the present, however, the BBC is financed by a receiver licence payable by every household in the UK that receives and watches an authorised broadcast signal. The licence fee was raised in December 1981 to £46 for a colour set and £15 for a black-and-white set. The previous fees were £34 and £12. The increase is to last three years, until December 1984. Since then the government has indicated that the BBC's 'Window on the World' satellite service would be financed by a supplementary licence fee; initially, at least.

11

	Colour	Black and white
Denmark	72	43
Sweden	63	48
Belgium	62	43
Norway	62	50
Switzerland	60	60
Finland	59/50	34/25
Austria	57	57
UK	46	15
France	40	26
Ireland	39	24
Germany, FR	37	37
Italy	35	19
Netherlands	31	31

The table gives the licence fees for the main European countries. Finland has two categories because some programmes can be received only in some parts of the country.

THE IBA

3.3.1. The Independent Broadcasting Authority operates under the Broadcasting Acts, the most significant of which are the 1973 Broadcasting Act and the 1980 Broadcasting Act. These Acts allow the IBA to provide television and local sound broadcasting services. The 1980 Act extended the IBA's life to 31 December 1996 with the possibility of further extension to 2001. Within the context of the Broadcasting Acts it has always been in the IBA's power to decide the broad organisation of its TV and radio services. The decision to have regional ITV companies, for instance, was entirely an IBA decision. That pattern has remained the chief element of ITV, even though the regional companies differ greatly in size and influence. There are now five major (or 'network') companies (Thames, London Weekend Television, Central, Yorkshire Television and Granada) who plan the ITV network, and ten regional, smaller companies. Together, the Independent Television Companies Association (ITCA) own ITN and ITV Publications.

3.3.2. The IBA has just completed an arduous round of agreeing new contracts with ITV programme companies, the first for 13 years. The regional contracts run from 1 January 1982 to 31 December 1989, although extensions to the early 1990s are more than likely. The breakfast-time contract runs from 1 May 1983 to 30 April 1991; that 1991 date could well become the termination date for all ITV contracts.

3.3.3. It is possible that the date of ITV's breakfast-time service will be brought forward to early 1983 or even to the end of 1982. The TV-AM company, headed by Peter Jay, has always wanted to start as soon as it was ready, which could be autumn 1982. The delay is the more infuriating because in March 1982 the BBC, as expected, decided to produce its own breakfast-time show, which will start in early spring 1983, beating TV-AM by several months. It is likely that the provision of two breakfast-time shows will increase the total audience watching TV; but the results of this competition will be less revenue for TV-AM. The competition for audiences is given some irony by the feeling among many people that breakfast-time television is not a priority in British television over the next few years and that the BBC is only providing its service because of the threat of TV-AM.

3.3.4. The 1980 Broadcasting Act authorised the IBA to operate a 'second television channel', Channel Four, which will start broadcasting in November 1982. This new channel will be used to provide one service for England, Scotland and Northern Ireland and a combined English and Welsh language service for Wales. The main English service will be operated by the Channel Four Television Company, an IBA subsidiary whose chairman and directors are appointed by the IBA. The company will be financed by annual subscriptions from the ITV companies who will in turn gain revenue from selling Channel Four's advertising time. In financial and cultural terms Channel Four is likely to be the country's most significant TV development for several years.

3.3.5. In Wales the service will be provided by Sianel Pedwar Cymru (Welsh Fourth Channel Authority) which was set up by Parliament. S4C will receive a payment of about £20 million a year from the ITV companies (some of which might otherwise be paid to the Treasury as levy). After covering its administrative costs (put at £2 million) S4C will spend about £18 million buying programmes from HTV, other ITV companies and independent producers. These sources are reckoned to supply 12 hours of programmes a week. In addition, BBC Wales will provide 10 hours of programmes a week financed by the national licence fee (the BBC has not put a price on its contribution but ITV reckon it to be about £18–19 million a year). These 22 hours constitute the Welsh language element. The major part of the channel will be the 50 hours of English language programmes provided by Channel Four without charge. Harlech Television (HTV), by using the ITV network regional programme tariff, has calculated the cost of these extra programmes at £6 million a year.

3.4. The licensing of Channel Four completed the UK's allocation of UHF frequencies. Under ITU agreement the UK also has an allocation of VHF bands. These VHF allocations were used for the original 405-line black-and white services of BBC-1 and ITV (while BBC-2 started at the higher frequencies, in colour). They are still used to transmit BBC-1 and ITV but the transmitters are being shut down in stages, with the last VHF transmitter scheduled to close by 1986. Several options are available for the future use of these frequencies. The transmitters may be re-engineered to provide one national 625-line colour TV service. Mobile radio is another likely contender (illustrating again the interdependence of all services using the radio spectrum). Mobile radio is a growth industry and, unlike television, totally dependent on wireless telegraphy. Another possibility is for a fuller teletext service.

14

4 Distribution: Satellite Delivery

4.1.1. There is a third group of frequencies, the super high frequencies (SHF), which have been allocated to broadcasting and assigned to the UK but whose use has not yet been licensed. These are the 'satellite' frequencies, at 12 GHz.

4.1.2. Satellite communications combine two distinct features that in the public's mind too often overlap. Space and spacecraft are the mysterious features; the exploitation a matter of high technology and high adventure. But these aerospace matters are not directly relevant to communications policy. The other feature of space communications, the electronics payload, is much more significant. It is also mundane and functionally simple. There is no essential difference between a broadcasting relay station on top of a hill and a broadcasting relay atop a satellite. The signals are received, adjusted and retransmitted in exactly the same manner. To avoid interference, terrestrial stations and space stations use different frequencies, and the long distances travelled by space signals require careful planning. But the principle is the same. The differences between terrestrial retransmission and satellite retransmission are not technical but concern the way in which the signals are used.

4.1.3. It is now possible to use a satellite to beam TV signals over a very wide area of the Earth's territory so that they can be picked up by either very small receivers or by slightly larger receivers and retransmitted through a cable system. Predicting the area covered by a particular satellite involves a number of variables. There is a direct mathematical relationship, however, between the power of a satellite, its beam, its frequency, and the size (and cost) of the ground dish receiver. The current generation of US satellites (called domestic satellites, or domsats) use 4 GHz frequencies to broadcast to dish antennas that are 3–9 metres in diameter. The next generation of advanced satellites now being developed in Europe (and also in North America and Japan) use the 12/14 GHz band and, with their extra wattage, can deliver signals to antennas as small as 90 cm. or even 60 cm. in diameter. This new generation of satellites, delivering five or as much as seven kilowatts of power, are generally called 'large' or 'advanced' satellites.

4.1.4. An ITU World Administrative Radio Conference held in 1977 agreed an international plan for satellite broadcasting which assigned five 12 GHz satellite TV channels to virtually every country in Europe, Asia and Africa. The Americas will hold a similar conference in 1983. It is therefore possible for each country to license the use of up to five more TV channels, beamed by satellite into its own territory and, to varying degrees and often significantly, into neighbouring countries as well.

4.1.5. The 1977 plan was designed to provide 'national services' that, for a national broadcasting organisation, would cover the organisation's own national territory but not any neighbouring territory (although few engineers in Geneva had thought deeply whether satellites were appropriate to such national restrictions). The plan was based on contemporary technology; its aim was to provide a high quality TV signal that could be picked up by a 'standard' 90 cm. dish throughout each national territory. But satellite R & D since 1977 has meant that a 1982 60 cm. dish can pick up as good a picture as the old 1977 90 cm. dishes. The actual coverage of a satellite designed to WARC-77 specifications would now extend over a wide area, from 60 cm. dishes in the country itself to 90 cm. dishes nearby to 3 metre dishes on the 'other side' of Europe. The smaller dishes would be owned by individual households; the larger ones would feed cable systems serving 'community' networks, hotels, entire towns, etc. The ITU has tried to erect a legal definition of both 'individual' and 'community' reception and has agreed that both kinds qualify for the title of 'direct' reception. But these 'technology-based' definitions do not work, and are not reflected in any national or EEC legislation. It is better, when using the term 'broadcasting satellite', to ignore the dubious distinctions of 'direct', 'individual' and 'community', and describe the service, if necessary, by reference to the cost of the dish required to receive the signal. If large numbers of people can afford to receive the signal then the satellite is effectively broadcasting. This suggested definition replaces the ITU's technical and regulatory criterion with a marketplace criterion.

4.1.6. The 1977 plan could lead to a theoretical 175 channels; but such an explosion is very improbable. Earlier plans for UHF broadcasting allow many more channels than are actually used; indeed, the UK is the only European country to take up its allocation of four UHF channels. In fact, the large number of dormant UHF channels could be taken to imply that there is no demand for more TV channels and that the satellite channels will remain unused. This argument would seem to be fallacious for two reasons: (1) whereas most European broadcasting organisations have been financed primarily by national licence fees (and thus restricted), the new satellite services will be commercially self-supporting through advertising or cable subscriptions; (2) satellite broadcasting is inherently international, and most services will be able to exploit this facility.

4.2.1. After a slow start the UK began to think quite actively about satellite TV. The Home Office published a report, *Direct Broadcasting by Satellite,* in May 1981, which laid down five options of which the middle one, 'a modest but early start', seemed the most favoured by the Home Office and the Department of Industry. The option implied two or three channels and a launch in 1986. It must be said that originally the Home Office did not seem overly keen on satellite broadcasting. It felt that the current ecology of four terrestrial channels is a good one, and should not be threatened. It asked, where is the demand for more television? Who wants satellite TV? The answer, of course, is not the public; the public never wants anything until it is asked. But there are powerful lobbies.

4.2.2. The BBC has argued strongly for two channels since 1980. One channel would have a mix of the best of BBC-1 and BBC-2, partly for those people who cannot pick up the existing terrestrial signals, and partly for those who want a second chance to see programmes. The second channel, in the words of Brian Wenham, Controller BBC-2, would be 'quite fancy' and provide a new premium service paid for by viewers' subscriptions. The BBC position is a logical derivation of its constitution and financial circumstances. It is not so logically a policy of public service. If the idea of public service was conceived differently, and enshrined in different constitutional/financial conditions, the BBC might act differently.

4.2.3. The IBA was less committed because it was embroiled in the launch of Channel Four and TV-AM, and feared that the currently bullish advertising revenue might be too much threatened by more commercial channels. Throughout 1980 and 1981 the Authority's stance was cautious and questioning. It asked, did the UK want more broadcast TV? (implying the answer, no). It shared Home Office views about the possibility of threats to the existing ecology of broadcasting. And it raised the institutional conundrum.

4.2.4. Speaking at the conference on satellite broadcasting organised by *The Economist* and the IIC in November 1981, Colin Shaw, Director of Television IBA, said that it might be in the national interest to create a new organisation to regulate British satellite services. 'I am not greatly in favour of creating new institutions with new bureaucracies. But equally, I am not much in favour of so distorting existing institutions in order to avoid making new ones that their original purposes are lost or seriously affected.' It is notable that the 1981 French (Moinot) commission on broadcasting came to the same conclusion, and proposed a new public body to regulate satellite broadcasting. Mr Shaw also said: 'I wait to be convinced that, at a time when many people are showing signs of wishing to draw back from the mass, from the large-scale, of seeking the local and the domestic in preference to the international and grandiose, satellites can sufficiently narrow their range to reflect at least this element in the contemporary mood.'

4.2.5. A few months later the New Year saw the IBA in more bullish form. No longer was the BBC making all the running. The IBA's case, made in its third submission to the Home Office, said that as satellite broadcasting was a commercially risky operation the IBA was the more appropriate authority to manage its introduction. Most, but not all, the ITCA companies agreed with the IBA proposal. At the end of February the Authority and its friends marshalled a new offensive. Lord Aylestone, a former chairman, wrote a persuasive letter to *The Times* saying that the public issues should be fully debated before a decision was made. He suggested the BBC was becoming too big. Two days later, a *Times* leader said that the BBC's virtue should be to be 'distinctive not dominant'. But it was too late. The Home Secretary had already made up his mind.

4.2.6. There were several reasons for the Government's haste. The aerospace industry had mounted a powerful lobby, British Aerospace has claims to being Europe's leading satellite manufacturer, since it has more contracts than any other company from the European Space Agency and Eutelsat, and also has the EEC's largest share of US subcontracts. It has led worldwide development of the new generation of advanced, large satellites specially designed for direct satellite broadcasting. This technical and managerial expertise was known in Whitehall. The Secretary of State for Industry has appointed George Jefferson, then head of BAe, to become chairman of the new British Telecom. What's more, British Aerospace had combined with GEC-Marconi to form a new consortium especially for the construction of a UK broadcast satellite system. British Telecom was a third partner, and Rothschilds merchant bank was ready with the money. Throughout 1981 this United Satellite Ltd (no relation to the US company of the same name) carried out several market surveys and met with ministers and officials.

4.2.7. There were other voices urging government support for satellite broadcasting. If the BBC represented one side of the broadcasting industry, Satellite Television plc could be said to represent the other. The leading spirit of SATV, and the evangelist of satellite broadcasting in Europe, is Brian Haynes, a former Thames TV producer, who was the first to realise the potential of satellites to provide new, different kinds of television to new audiences. Brian Haynes advised first Thames TV, then ITCA and then an industry group before setting up SATV in 1980. Its thrust is to exploit any satellite that has spare TV capacity. Brian Haynes began by looking at the European Space Agency's Orbital Test Satellite, and gradually persuaded the governing body, Eutelsat, that SATV should be allowed to use OTS to set up a 'fixed telecommunications' link between the UK and Malta. Such links are normally used for telephone, telex, etc., circuits; but it is in the nature of radio waves that they propagate without regard to national boundaries, and the UK-Malta signals can actually be received throughout Western Europe. Brian Haynes had shown that it could be done; that space was a new resource that was ready for exploration and beneficial use.

4.2.8. There was, finally, the broad imperative of industrial strategy. At the end of 1981 the present government passed its midterm mark and it now has to face the prospect of an election in the next eighteen months (the latest time, almost certain to be ruled out, is the spring of 1985). Fortuitously, 1982 is the year of Information Technology, and the many ministers with responsibility for industry, employment and trade saw the new industrial technologies as a likely source of new jobs and new wealth – and electoral gains. The building of satellites and accompanying equipment (not to mention the making of programmes) and the construction of a national cable network have become part of the Government's strategy to revitalise the economy and the hallmark of its election campaign.

4.2.9. Several government departments and agencies are involved in the decisions on a British satellite system. The 'lead' department is the Home Office, which has exclusive responsibilities for the licensing of broadcasting uses. It is up to the Home Office to decide the nature of the licence, and to ensure, if it wishes, an integrated policy for broadcasting by terrestrial and satellite transmitters. However, two other departments are also involved. The Department of Industry, through its Information Technology Division and its Space Division, has a twofold concern with the industrial, aerospace aspects. It was significant that Britain's £70 million investment in L-Sat, which is Europe's experimental regional broadcasting satellite, was announced not by the Home Secretary or any Home Office Minister but by Kenneth Baker MP, Minister of State for Information Technology in the Department of Industry.

4.2.10. The satellite policy announced by William Whitelaw on 4 March has three main strands. The first is the decision 'in principle' to have a British satellite broadcasting system designed to the technical standards agreed at the 1977 World Administrative Radio Conference (WARC). The satellite will be built by British Aerospace which must be confirmed as Europe's leading satellite manufacturer.

4.2.11. The second theme is the issue of ownership and control. The chain of regulation from government to user can be constructed in many different ways, and can be long or short. The issue of licensing can be resolved by setting up many different kinds of organisations; so can the issue of franchising and use. It seems the BBC could provide a satellite service without any alteration to its Charter and Licence; the assumption is correct given that the BBC would be constrained to provide a certain kind of service. The IBA, however, would require an alteration to its Licence and probably legislative changes to the Broadcasting Acts. A new organisation, of course, would require a new licence. It seems, therefore, that the Home Secretary will have to face, sooner rather than later, the problem of licences for satellite broadcasting, and that the arrangement with the BBC only postpones the day when new procedures must be set up. The Home Secretary could issue a direct licence as he has done for the cable projects but such direct action not only contradicts the cherished tradition of an independent public authority but also involves the Secretary of State in matters which he acknowledges should be delegated. There are several possibilities. The conventional solution would be to set up a new public authority (the Annan principle). Alternatively the government could extend, if necessary, the powers of an existing authority. It could devise a body (committee, commission, agency, etc.) that would not have the traditionally powerful, almost mythic, halo of 'authority' but which would be competent to issue licences and monitor usage. If these matters need legislation then no final decision can be expected before the 1982/3 session at the earliest, although it is worth remembering that the Channel Four company started work before the legislation was passed; it hired its directors and staff as 'consultants'.

4.2.12. For the time being the Home Secretary has chosen to rely upon the BBC's existing licence, and to devolve his responsibilities to the consortium that will build the satellite which, in negotiation with the BBC (and others?), sets the necessary standards and agreements. The lack of regulation at this stage is markedly different from the government's positive intervention by legislation in the establishment of terrestrial networks. It gives considerable potential power to the United Satellites consortium set up by British Aerospace, GEC-Marconi and British Telecom. United Satellites looks like the clear favourite to win

20

the contract for the system (which will probably consist of one operational in-orbit spacecraft, one in-orbit spare and one spare on the ground) and with Rothschilds merchant bank is well advanced in raising the necessary capital. In his speech Mr Whitelaw spoke of the consortium but gave no details whatsoever, not even indicating how it would be chosen, or how regulated. He did indicate, however, that the consortium would be given wide powers to organise its own financial affairs and set technical standards.

4.2.13. One of the more interesting proposals has come from the Channel Four company, which sees itself as a useful model: an intelligent compromise between authoritative control, commercial ambition and creative freedom. The IBA has accepted this argument, not surprisingly, and is also supporting the idea of a similar subsidiary to run an ITCA satellite channel. But the principle goes wider and could be used outside the ITV arena.

4.2.14. The third issue is the allocation of the channels. Similarly to most other European countries the UK was assigned five 12 GHz satellite channels, and an orbital position of 31° west, at the 1977 WARC. The UK channels are 4, 8, 12, 16 and 20. It is a matter of national convenience how many and which of these channels are actually used.

4.2.15. The Home Secretary has decided to allocate two channels immediately and the remainder 'when demand justified it'. They will be run by the BBC. He said that DBS must develop in a way that is consistent with our existing broadcasting arrangements, especially as regards supervision by a broadcasting authority and 'maintenance of proper programme standards'. That clearly means the BBC and IBA, and the BBC has won the draw. The Home Secretary justified his decision by saying the BBC was further advanced in its planning; and that a BBC operation would require no new statutory arrangements or legislation, whereas an IBA operation might require both.

4.2.16. The argument is not altogether convincing. There is a full four years before the satellite can be launched and that is surely time enough even for a brand new organisation to be set up, and the necessary legislation passed. Channel Four needed only two years. The government's decision to favour the BBC has been strongly criticised by the IBA and some ITV companies and by a number of people who feel the Home Secretary has acted rather too hastily. It has also been said that the speed with which organisations make proposals (and the BBC, being a monolithic institution, can usually move faster than the IBA and

ITV) should not be a major criterion in the formulation of national policy on such important matters.

4.2.17. The BBC has confirmed that it wishes to provide two satellite services as originally proposed. The first, subscription, channel would consist mainly of feature films, including films newly released. The BBC hopes to be able to buy films on first release, without any time restriction. The subscription channel would also have major music and theatrical events; and sport and popular entertainment. The channel would be coded and available only to those who paid a monthly fee.

4.2.18. The second channel would be a 'Window on the World', featuring 'the best television from around the world', including repeats of programmes first broadcast on BBC-1 and BBC-2 and, the BBC hopes, ITV and Channel Four as well. The inclusion of 'programmes from around the world' is a recent addition to the channel's proposed contents. The BBC hopes to co-produce many of these programmes with an international flavour. The reason for the new emphasis is the BBC's new awareness of the fact of spillover. Many of these international programmes will no doubt be designed to maximise the channel's appeal in mainland Europe. This second channel will be financed initially by a supplementary licence fee payable by those who wish to receive it (rather as colour broadcasting was financed by a 'colour' licence fee). The BBC hopes that eventually both satellite channels will be funded mainly from the pay-TV service. As for its financial plans, the BBC does not seem to put much weight on its own projections on audiences and income. It is aware that the success of the service depends largely on the growth of cable systems; and that, while outside the BBC's control, is likely to be rapid enough to provide a substantial audience.

4.2.19. Most professional and public attention is focused on satellite television. It is fairly certain, however, that the number of satellite TV channels will be outnumbered by the number of satellite radio channels, because radio requires relatively little bandwidth. The BBC proposals would like to use the UK satellite for digital transmission of high-quality music services. Another possibility is a satellite version of the BBC World Service (although the BBC is also considering renting a Luxembourg channel for the World Service, since its satellite covers a greater territory in Eastern Europe). These proposals are separate from the sound channels that would accompany the TV channels, and which could provide two or more different language tracks.

4.2.20. The IBA was disappointed at the government's decision. It liked neither the method (a ministerial announcement, without any

prior parliamentary or public debate) nor the result. It argued that the
IBA and ITV system was a more appropriate organisation than the BBC
to provide a new, risky commercial TV service. It also said that Channel
Four (an IBA subsidiary, financed by advertising collected by the ITV
companies who then pay a commensurate 'subscription' to the IBA and
Channel Four) might provide a useful model for the operation of a
satellite service. It proposed three ITV services: a pay-TV service, a 'Best
of British' service, taking programmes from all four channels; and a
pan-European service. The IBA may have lost the first round but it is
unlikely to be deprived permanently. The Home Secretary said that the
government attaches importance to the participation of commercial
television companies and Alasdair Milne, Director General designate
BBC, has said he feels the government would be 'very uneasy' if the
satellite service started without an ITV presence.

4.2.21. It is not yet decided what kind of satellite will be built for the
new system although the name, Halley, seems to be accepted. British
Aerospace has two options: a version of the European Communications
Satellites (ECS), the first of which will be launched this year for the
European Space Agency; and a version of the L-Sat now being built for
a 1986 launch, also for the ESA. Both satellites could easily be
engineered to fit WARC-77 specifications. But they have key differences.
The ECS is smaller and weaker and can provide a maximum of two
channels to WARC-77 specifications; on the other hand it is cheaper to
build (but the two-channel capacity means that the user rental is £15
million per channel per year) and can be ready more quickly. The
L-Sat is bigger and much more powerful and can provide five full
WARC-77 channels; the annual rental might be £10 million per
channel. Even minimum ITV involvement would necessitate an L-Sat.
So would any involvement by British Telecom's UK or international
telecommunication services. From both standpoints it looks as if the
larger satellite is the more likely.

OTHER COUNTRIES

4.3.1. The plans of neighbouring countries for satellite broadcasting
are relevant partly because the development of each new service and
new market helps overall. There is also a more basic reason. Satellites
are the most international of the new media. Just as listeners to 'pirate'
radio stations did not care whether the programmes came from a ship
in the North Sea or an old fort in the Thames estuary, and just as
viewers to ITV don't care where *Brideshead Revisited* was financed,
produced and made; so tomorrow's viewers won't know and won't care
whether the bulk of their TV programmes come from London, Munich,
Paris or Hollywood; by satellite, cable or even terrestrial transmission.

There are several plans for satellite broadcasting in Europe, mostly at a tentative stage, and all likely to be altered as the market develops (a detailed analysis can be found in the IIC report, *Satellite Broadcasting in Western Europe*, May 1982).

4.3.2. France and West Germany have a joint project to launch two pre-operational satellites, to be followed by national systems. The German satellite is scheduled to be launched first, in 1985, and the French satellite six months later. These dates could well slip and the first European satellite service (excluding SATV) may not start before 1986. The Franco-German project has grown out of the two countries' long-standing collaboration in technology and industrial development and this concord at the industrial level has not been matched with any similar agreement on the satellites' purposes and uses. The broadcasters in both countries are either indifferent or wanting to experiment with services that cannot easily be accommodated in the existing policy framework. There is not much agreement about the configuration of even the pre-operational satellites.

4.3.3. President Giscard d'Estaing was thinking of using the French TdF satellite to distribute the two national channels of TF-1 and A-2. The fate of the third channel was undecided but it was generally assumed to be intended for Europe No. 1, a private radio station, part owned by French state holdings, that broadcasts into France. Initially, President Mitterand also wanted to use the satellite to duplicate existing terrestrial transmission of FR-1 and A-2; but the third channel was more of a problem. The socialists did not look with favour on the highly commercial peripheral stations. One possible solution was proposed by the government's Moinot Commission, which recommended two channels with a mix of TF-1 and A-2 and a third channel of special programmes aimed at a European audience. However, the draft bill announced on 1 April 1982 makes no firm recommendation. Satellites are not a top priority in France at the moment. The public is much more concerned with terrestrial broadcasting; especially the quality of peak-time television, and the growth of private, local radio stations.

4.3.4. In West Germany the situation is also confused. The Franco-German agreement was signed by the Bonn federal government; but broadcasting is the responsibility not of the federal government but of the Länder regional states. The Bonn government and the Länder governments have often disagreed about the management of broadcasting. The picture is complicated by the political tension inside the Bonn coalition and the recent tendency in Land elections in favour of the opposition parties. It is not surprising that both the federal government and the Land-based broadcasting organisations have not yet been able to generate the kind of imaginative innovation needed for satellite development. The existing policy may be described as a least worst solution. It has been generally agreed that the pre-operational satellite would have three channels, of which two channels would be used to distribute the regular A R D and Z D F national services, while the third channel would be used for 12 or 16 hi-fi radio services. But, just as France is now looking seriously at the possibility of a pan-European service, so several A R D stations and Z D F are discussing the possibility of a pan-European service. These services may involve just Austria and Switzerland or all Western Europe.

4.3.5. It is characteristic of satellite broadcasting that, for a small country, the satellite easily reaches more people outside the country's own territory than inside it. For some years, therefore, Radio-Télé-Luxembourg, which has Luxembourg's sole broadcasting licence, has been investigating ways of providing a European satellite service. It hopes to start an operational service in three languages but political difficulties *vis-à-vis* the Paris and Bonn governments have so far prevented it from taking the plunge. However, both neighbours are now less hostile. The French Prime Minister has withdrawn his country's main objections and Germany, too, seems less militantly opposed. At one stage, the German newspaper and periodical publishers proposed a joint venture; but the scheme had little financial benefit and no political advantage, and has now been put to one side.

4.3.6. Switzerland, like Luxembourg, can benefit from its satellite's wide international coverage, and its location at the centre of Europe makes it an ideal candidate for a multi-national satellite service. The most active proponent has been the Tel-Sat consortium, formed by some U K companies (now withdrawn) and Swiss publishers. Tel-Sat proposed first a five and then a three channel system, but the government saw no need for haste and has not responded. Meanwhile the national broadcasting organisation has countered by putting its priorities on the expansion of cable networks. The government is unlikely to make a decision for some time; certainly not before the media commission reports later this year.

4.3.7. These national plans of France, West Germany, Luxembourg and Switzerland (and the U K) are the forerunners. But national plans tell only half the story, if that. The point and justification of a satellite system is the service it provides, and satellite services will be inherently international. Several new groupings along cultural or linguistic lines are likely to take shape and would indeed be the most sensible exploitation of satellite technology. One such grouping has been discussed for many years in Scandinavia. The Nordic countries (Denmark, Finland, Iceland, Norway, Sweden) have been trying to set up a Nordsat system which would serve all member countries and the 1977 WARC makes special provision for such a service. Disagreements over costs and the cultural objectives have prevented Nordsat from gaining any real political momentum. It is possible, however, that Sweden's national Tele-X system might lead to a regional system; or, conversely, that Tele-X might provide a regional service.

4.3.8. There are several interesting plans for full European-wide services. The chief protagonist is the European Space Agency, an intergovernmental organisation of eleven European states and Canada. The ESA already has an experimental Orbital Test Satellite (OTS) in orbit that can deliver TV to three-metre antenna dishes throughout Europe. The OTS, which is now being used by SATV to deliver TV not only to Malta but in fact throughout Europe, is expected to run out of fuel by the end of 1982. However, the ESA is developing two other satellite systems that can deliver TV throughout Europe. One is to be fully operational, the other is experimental.

4.3.9. The European Communications Satellite (ECS) series of five satellites will be a fully operational, commercial system for Europe's national telecommunication authorities (e.g. British Telecom, Bundespost, PTT). The ECS satellite will be used for telecommunications of all kinds: telephone, telex, data and video. The video channels will be used by the European Broadcasting Union to link its member organisations in a new Eurovision network for the exchange of newsfilm and other Eurovision material. The channels will be wholly within the framework of the national telecommunications authorities; they are not intended for direct reception by the public. Indeed, the ECS system is not intended to provide direct TV transmission of any sort. But, technically, they can deliver TV if not to 60 cm. rooftop dishes then to the kind of larger dish that might be installed by a cable operator. Again, it is a question of regulation, not technical possibility.

4.3.10. The ESA is also developing an experimental satellite designed specifically for direct broadcasting. The L-Sat ('L' for large) can provide five TV channels to full WARC-77 specifications. The brunt of the cost of L-Sat is being born by the UK, which is paying £70 million, and Italy, which is paying the same. The remaining £70 million is being contributed by Austria, Belgium, Canada, Denmark, Netherlands and Spain.

4.3.11. The ESA satellites that are available are now being used to provide two quite different kinds of satellite broadcasting. One service, called 'Satellite', is produced by a commercial consortium (SATV); the other is being administered under the auspices of the European Broadcasting Union. The differences in the two services illustrate the changing nature of today's satellite plans.

4.3.12. The SATV company originated in an entrepreneurial determination to use satellites to provide television throughout Europe. Although registered in the UK in September 1980 (before most professional broadcasters had begun to treat satellites as a real possibility), SATV's first and still current aim has been to exploit existing satellites to distribute entertainment to continental cable systems. It is aiming at the continent's top 400 cable systems which in 1981 had over 4,500,000 subscribers. According to SATV that subscriber base would generate, on the most optimistic assumptions, a turnover after five years of £35 million and a profit of £29 million; on its most pessimistic projection turnover would be £13 million and profit £3.5 million. After many months of experimental transmission, by May 1982 SATV was close to starting a more regular service. Its programmes included several LWT comedy series (*Please Sir!*, *Within These Walls*, etc.) and YTV's *Hadleigh;* about 30% of the material is foreign. Polaroid, Kelloggs, Wrangler and Schweppes are among the advertisers.

4.3.13. Four crucial factors will influence SATV's future. The first is the availability of satellites. SATV has a thoroughly international attitude towards hardware. It will apply to book time on any satellite that is available. So far, it has used only ESA satellites and when OTS runs out of fuel it hopes to be able to use the first ECS. With these satellites a cable system in France needs a 1.8 metre dish; in Finland, a 4 metre dish. The second factor is the spread of cable. SATV is aiming solely at cable markets; more cable subscribers means more revenue with no increase in costs. Third, competitive satellite systems may expand the total market and alter SATV's market share. Fourth, the UK government's decision to allow the SATV service to be received in the UK would increase revenue substantially. At present, SATV is careful not even to include UK reception in its published plans; but both SATV and UK cable companies see benefits in having the service legally receivable throughout the country. At the beginning of 1982 only Finland, Norway and Malta were redistributing the service.

4.3.14. Whereas SATV is a newcomer to television the other current service is being provided under the auspices of the European Broadcasting Union (EBU), the well-established professional association of European broadcasting organisations. A number of EBU committees have been looking at the possibility of a pan-European direct broadcast satellite channel for some years. Towards the end of 1981 several people within EBU member organisations agreed to set up a series of five European programme experiments. The first experiment using OTS will be organised by the IBA on 24–30 May. Later experiments will be held by RAI, Italy; ORF, Austria; NOS, Netherlands; and ARD, West Germany. Each experiment will involve a daily schedule from 6–11p.m. The signals will be scrambled and so cannot be watched by the public. The IBA is taking the lead role in the experiment and Neville Clarke, Senior Television Programme Officer, is Head of the Operations Group that is responsible for planning and co-ordination. The BBC is not so involved but has offered the assistance of Kingswood Warren, its technical research centre.

4.3.15. Satellite systems are expensive and complicated and except for SATV no European services are likely to be operational for several years. But by 1986 people in the UK will be able to pick up several satellite TV services. The number of channels receivable depends on several factors:

- UK government policies
- other government policies
- the existence of cable systems
- the power of satellites and ground receivers
- the integration of advertising markets
- copyright management
- the viewer's location

Most factors are imponderable and will remain so until the first services start broadcasting. The development of cable is crucial. So is the development of programme services attractive enough to be worth paying for?

5 Distribution: Cables and Wires

5.1. The third major form of transmission system is by cable and wires. The chief characteristic which distinguishes these services is the way in which the signal enters the user's home; it does not hinge on the transmission process as a whole. Just as all BBC and IBA signals travel by cable before being broadcast, so most cable signals are broadcast before they are cabled. The interrelation is a reminder that the UK, in common with other industrial countries, already has a vast network of wired communications that is separate from, although contiguous with, the known cable television systems. The British Telecom network is conventionally known as the telephone network because that was its first purpose and remains its chief use. Most households are wired up to this narrowband network. The wire, of course, is often primitive and limited in capacity. But it exists and British Telecom is spending some £3 million a day in improvements. The integration or interconnection of the public switched network and the private cable networks is one of the great policy issues of this decade. Innovation in services is coming from both British Telecom and the private cable companies. British Telecom invented Prestel, the world's first wired videotex system, and is now developing a host of new services, mainly involving data exchange but also providing facsimile and video. The cable companies are concentrating their energies on entertainment and on services designed for the home rather than the office. This paper covers both lines of development; but it focuses on those developments that affect the individual user, and its concern with media, with content, emphasises the potential of wideband cable networks.

5.2.1. The Home Office licenses about 2,291 cable operators (all 1980 figures) to relay broadcasting services by cable. These systems pass a total of 4 million households and provide TV to 2,592,000 households (13.8% of TV households) of which 1,483,000 (7.9%) are fed by commercial companies. The licences are controlled by the Home Secretary under the 1949 Wireless Telegraphy Act, section 1. Each operator has to complete a Technical Questionnaire and agree to Technical Conditions and Performance Standards. If these are satisfactory the Home Office issues a Licence for a Broadcast Relay (including Communal Aerial) Apparatus. The licences and fees are laid in front of Parliament every year but they do not involve legislation and are not debated. The licence authorises the holder to receive and relay (2.1.a) 'sound programmes from authorised broadcasting stations wherever situated' and (2.1.b) 'television programmes from authorised broadcasting stations in the UK, the Channel Islands or the Isle of Man or, with the consent of the Secretary of State, from authorised broadcasting stations wherever situated'.

5.2.2. It is an important condition of the licence that the cable operator must relay all services that are locally available (the 'must carry' clause). For sound services, under schedule 2, section 1(a) 'the licensee shall ensure that all the programmes broadcast by the BBC for general reception throughout the UK which the system is capable of distributing are distributed; (b) the licensee may distribute, in addition, such other programmes broadcast by an authorised broadcasting station and which the system is capable of distributing as he may select.' There is further provision for carrying BBC and IBA local services. For television services, the same principles apply. Under schedule 3, section 1, 'if there is available for the reception of users of the system programmes broadcast by the BBC the licensee shall ensure that all programmes broadcast by the Corporation which the system is capable of distributing are distributed at all such times as they are broadcast.' The situation with IBA programmes is complicated by the fact of different regional services, but the principles are similar. The licence specifies which stations may be carried.

5.2.3. Every cable service needs this basic licence under the 1949 Act if it is to provide a relay service. It can also apply for other licences to supply other kinds of service. With very few exceptions, the applications would be refused; but there have been exceptions. In the early 1970s (when broadcasting was regulated by the Ministry of Posts and Telecommunications) the ministry did issue licences under the 1969 Post Office Act, part IV, to five cable companies to provide some community services in addition to the basic relay services. The five companies in Bristol, Greenwich, Sheffield, Swindon and Wellingborough generally provided a few hours daily of local community programmes. The local programmes were often interesting but after a few years all the licensees (except Greenwich) stopped their services for financial reasons. In 1980 the Home Secretary decided to offer special licences to another small group of cable companies to allow them to provide pay-TV. These licences will be discussed below. Finally, a cable company can apply for a licence to offer data and textual information as a 'value added' service. The company would require a licence from British Telecom (or the Secretary of State for Industry) under the Telecommunications Act 1981, section 15. These slight derogations from the central Post Office (now British Telecom) monopoly have not been important except at the local level; their effect on government policy has been slight. The cable companies have not been enthusiastic because the licences have been strictly worded (especially in their restrictions on programmes and advertising) and of temporary duration.

5.3.1. The pay-TV operations licensed in 1981/82 might have been more substantial but recent events in the national political arena have ensured that they, too, will have a negligible effect on future policy. Nevertheless, it is worth describing them in some detail because they are relevant to the decisions the government will take in autumn 1982.

5.3.2. The licences were announced by the Home Secretary in the House of Commons on 10 November 1980:

(a) Licensees may show only feature films which have been granted a registration certificate by the British Board of Film Censors (the film industry's self-regulatory body). Films registered for public exhibition in a cinema in this country may be shown only after an interval of at least 12 months from the date of such registration. No films of category 'X' (unsuitable for persons under 18) may be shown before 10 p.m. A film which has been refused permission for exhibition in cinemas in a particular area may not be shown over subscription television in that area. The same requirements regarding the proportion of films of British or EEC origin will be applied in the pilot scheme as apply to showing in cinemas.

(b) Licensees may not seek exclusive rights to show sporting and entertainment events of national importance.

(c) Advertising will not be permitted.

(d) Licensees will be required to submit their programme schedules to the Home Office in advance.

(e) Licensees will be required to conduct research into public reactions to the subscription service, to monitor progress and to submit an account each year of the volume and nature of any complaints received and of any action taken in consequence.

The Home Secretary also intends to require an account each year of any programmes of local community interest which have been shown in the subscription service.

5.3.3. It is noteworthy that the Home Secretary did not follow the recommendation of the Annan Report (1977) nor of the Labour Government's white paper *Broadcasting* (1978) that the IBA (as a regional authority) be given responsibility for cable services. Instead, he chose to issue direct licences. He acknowledged in the Commons (10

31

November 1980) that 'it would not be practicable or appropriate [the order of problems is revealing] for the Home Office to supervise the programmes shown or to exercise the function of a broadcasting authority in the manner of the B B C or I B A.' To say that there might be a contradiction between the Secretary of State's requirement to see programme schedules in advance and his decision not to 'supervise the programmes shown' is perhaps to quibble. It is certainly possible to do one without the other. Yet the experience of the I B A has taught us to be very precise and very explicit about the responsibility and duties of the regulator and the programme-maker when it comes to programme content. Is pay-T V so very different?

5.3.4. The seven organisations providing pay-T V in various areas, some sharing programme suppliers and offering identical schedules, are as shown in the table.

Licensed operator	Programme supplier	Name of service	Location
Rediffusion	Rediffusion	Starview	Reading Pontypridd Hull Tunbridge Wells Burnley
Radio Rentals	Thorn-EMI Video Productions	Cinematel	Swindon Medway Towns (Chatham, Gillingham and Rochester)
British Telecom	SelecTV	SelecTV	Milton Keynes
Philips Cablevision	SelecTV	SelecTV	Tredegar Northampton
Visionhire Cable	BBC Enterprises	Showcable	London (various areas)
Cablevision	SelecTV	SelecTV	Wellingborough
Greenwich Cablevision	Greenwich Cablevision	Screentown	Greenwich

5.3.5. The cable systems that distribute these services pass 330,000 households. At the end of 1981 about 110,000 of the 330,000 households were subscribing to the regular cable service. The cable operators expect (and in some cases already have) about 10% of homes passed or

30% of homes subscribing to the relay service. This kind of penetration produces a total subscription population of about 30,000 households. It is not enough to make an industry. It has also been suggested that the policy framework of the projects, the services themselves and the expected research will not produce the necessary information for government to formulate a policy for the next stage. Even if it did, it might be too late.

5.4.1. The turning point was the Cabinet Office's publication of a report on *Cable Systems* (HMSO; ISBN 0 11 630821). The report was written by the government's Information Technology Advisory Panel whose secretariat is provided by the Information Technology Unit attached to the Cabinet Office. The report is directly significant in the UK's development of cable and satellites and the ministerial response has symbolised the government's new awareness of the politics of the new technologies, and their industrial importance.

5.4.2. The ITAP report made succinct criticism of the pilot projects: 'It would be more comfortable to follow the timescale envisaged in the current trials of subscription TV – one would feel more confident about the consequences of policy decisions – but to do so would almost certainly mean abandoning UK cable developments to overseas interests. The subscription TV trials are, frankly, three years too late.' William Whitelaw, the minister responsible, seems to have accepted the project's irrelevance. He acknowledged in the House of Commons on 22 March that 'A number of developments indicate the need for urgent decisions about the future role of cable sooner than the timescale implicit in the subscription television pilot schemes would permit'.

5.4.3. The Advisory Panel and the Information Technology Unit had been set up in July 1981 after a series of discussions in Whitehall, including Downing Street, about the best way to concentrate the government's collective mind on the opportunities of information technology. Several individual officials and advisers believed that the government needed an informed, powerful and public statement of the importance of cable systems. Their model was the ACARD report on information technology which has focussed attention in Whitehall and elsewhere on the importance of IT. The Information Technology Unit and the Advisory Panel were devised to do very much the same for the new technologies of communications.

5.4.4. The IT Unit was set up by the Prime Minister to handle 'interdepartmental IT policy matters' (House of Commons, 2 July 1981). She said it would be 'a principal link between the advisers and departments, will help to promote the use of IT within government and will seek to ensure the overall coherence of government policies towards I T, particularly insofar as they span the responsibility of more than one department'. The Unit has four members, drawn from the permanent civil service and the private sector: Brian Unwin, a former Treasury official; Roger Courtney, former secretary of A C A R D; Adrian Norman, from Arthur D. Little, and David Rayfield from Plessey. The Unit has worked in a positive way to ensure that all government departments are aware of all I T developments that might affect them and also to assist linkages between government, Whitehall and industry.

5.4.5. Something else was needed. The task of the I T Unit is essentially supportive. It has a certain status from its position in the Cabinet Office but it lacks the resources to initiate major policy proposals. The Prime Minister therefore complemented the Unit by setting up an Information Technology Advisory Panel (I T A P) for this more public task. Whereas the Unit consists of civil servants, who are debarred from giving their personal views, the members of the I T A P were selected specifically to give voice to their concerns and ambitions. The Prime Minister said that 'The Government fully recognise the importance of information technology (I T) for the future industrial and commercial success of the United Kingdom and the central role that Government must play in promoting its development and application. Government policies are already directed towards encouraging markets for I T products and services that will stimulate new, profitable business opportunities; and the Government see the effective application of I T as a powerful tool in raising the efficiency and quality of both private and public sector services. In order to ensure that Government policies and actions are securely based on a close appreciation of market needs and opportunities I am appointing a panel of I T advisors who will be able to advise me and my colleagues on all aspects of I T.'

5.4.6. The advisors are: Michael Aldrich (Managing Director, Rediffusion Computers Ltd); I. H. Cohen (Managing Director, Mullard Ltd); C. A. Davies (Managing Director, Information Technology Ltd); D. F. Hartley (Director, Cambridge University Computing Services); C. N. Read (Director, Inter-Bank Research Organisation); and G. C. Southgate (Chief Executive, Computer Service Division, British Oxygen Co Ltd).

5.4.7. In the composition of the I T A P the computer and electronics industries are heavily represented almost to the exclusion of other sectors. The I T Unit is concerned with broadcasting; yet the I T A P has little telecommunications expertise and no media interests whatsoever. It includes no one with a professional concern for the social and cultural aspects. An all-embracing remit might have slowed the work but these other concerns must be brought in at some stage.

5.5. The ITAP report, *Cable Systems*, recommends an interactive cable network with a minimum of 30 channels. Its proposals can be split into three separate categories: the industrial context; the cable system itself; and the regulatory implications. The first and last will be treated in Chapter 9. Here, we will deal with the cable network.

5.5.1. The detailed recommendations are:

(i) The Government should announce as soon as possible its approval for an early start on DBS services.* It should explicitly recognise the role of existing cable systems in providing an immediate market for DBS programmes and should give an undertaking that these will be allowed to distribute DBS transmission, where necessary – and subject to making suitable alternative arrangements – releasing them from the obligation to distribute terrestrial services. This will be a sign to cable interests that the Government sees a future for commercial cable systems; it may possibly help to retard current withdrawal strategies, but it will do nothing for their short-term prospects.

(ii) The Government should announce, by mid-1982, the broad outlines of its future policy towards cable systems, in order to allow the private sector to start planning new systems. We recommend that the policy should be to license new systems conforming to set technical standards without the present restrictions on programming (apart from obvious requirements on decency, sedition, etc. on which representatives of cable operators have already offered an undertaking). Such licensing could take place initially under existing legislation and administrative arrangements.

(iii) The Government should urgently review the implications of cable systems for the financing and regulation of broadcasting and should consider the need for a new statutory body to be the 'broadcasting authority' for cable systems. On the basis of this review, and investigation of the effects of different regulatory arrangements on potential private sector investment in cable systems, the Government should formulate and announce its detailed administrative and regulatory proposals. This announcement should be made as soon as possible and in any case by early 1983.

*The Home Secretary announced the Government's approval in principle for a two-channel operational DBS service starting in 1986 in a Parliamentary statement on 4 March 1982.

(iv) The Government should urge cable operators and programme providers to set up effective means of self-regulation, after the manner of the advertising and newspaper industries. This would help create public confidence and might well simplify any new regulatory arrangements.

(v) The Department of Industry should establish a technical working group including representatives of cable operators, the electronics industry and B T. This group would:

(a) examine alternative approaches to cable network design and recommend design standards for the United Kingdom,

(b) define the necessary detailed engineering standards, consistent with commercial viability, for that network.

It should complete its work during 1982.

The recommended design standards should offer maximum potential to the United Kingdom manufacturers and operators and should anticipate, to be compatible with, developments in communications technology. In particular, they should require systems to operate with the relevant constraints on usage and allocation of frequencies set by the Home Office (including F M radio channels in the 88-108 MHz band) and to be capable of incremental expansion beyond a defined minimum number of channels (perhaps 30) without disturbance to the final distribution network. Systems should be able to support a wide range of interactive services and should link with the packet-switched service of B T and other services offered by B T and alternative telecommunications networks. But the standards set should not prejudice commercial operations.

(vi) The Department of Industry should create an effective forum in which all those interested in cable systems can come together to unify their efforts to the benefit of the United Kingdom. To assist in this, the Department should rationalise its internal arrangements for considering cable issues which at present are spread over several divisions.

5.5.2. The cable network proposed by the I T A P is not the same kind of cable network now common in the U K nor is it the same kind of cable network now being installed in the U S A and Canada. Networking is a highly technical matter and cannot easily be explained in lay terms. It would be a pity. however, if the advantages and disadvantages of the proposed network were not fully known to policy-makers before the policy is formulated. Once in the ground, cables become expensive to change (imagine changing the national railway gauge).

36

5.5.3. The key parameter is bandwidth; the key criteria are cost, flexibility and capacity. Most UK cable systems consist of 'twisted pair' copper HF cable and have a very narrow bandwidth. The systems with four pairs of twisted wire (making about 70% of the total) can deliver only four channels; those with six pairs can deliver only six channels. There are two technologies that can provide much greater capacity (and more flexibility) at relatively lower cost. Coaxial cables, as widely used in the USA, also made of copper, are best used to provide up to 50 channels. Optical fibres, consisting of very thin pure glass, can transmit more channels more cheaply and more easily. Coaxial cable technology is well established and is used without exception in the USA and Canada. Optical fibres are still on test, although a few fibre networks are being laid in the UK (and elsewhere) as an integral part of the national switched narrowband (telephone) network. Optical fibres will probably become very much cheaper than all-copper cables. By 1985 British Telecom hopes to install about 20 optic fibre trunk links, mostly in south and central England, as a major part of its new 'Integrated Switched Digital Network' (ISDN) with which it hopes to improve substantially the networking of all kinds of electronic signals.

5.5.4. The thinking of the ITAP report on the shape of this network is very close to BT's own thoughts. As the ITAP report describes, the normal structure of a cable television system is that of a tree – with signals going in at the base of the trunk and spreading out through the branches to individual subscribers. Each subscriber simultaneously receives all signals. He selects a signal out of the welter that are arriving by tuning his TV set; if he has two TV sets he can receive two TV signals at the same time; and so on. This kind of tree structure is common in North America and is the basis of most existing UK cable systems.

5.5.5. But the ITAP proposes a different structure for the future. It is clear that most of the signals arriving at the subscriber's home are wasted. A 12-channel system can only be fully used by a household with 12 TV sets; a 48-channel service, providing data as well, would require a room full of sets and data displays. This redundancy, says the ITAP, is grossly inefficient and wasteful. Therefore, they propose a switched system. The main trunk lines (probably optic fibres) would deliver all the channels to a local switching point – a black box – which would serve 50–100 households. From then on, the cables to each subscriber would be smaller (probably coaxial, not optical) and capable of carrying only 30–40 MHz instead of the 350 MHz carried on the trunk cables. The subscriber would select a channel or channels by sending a return data signal from his house to the switching point which would then direct that channel down one of the subscriber's individual cables. The ITAP proposal is neat and cheap. It is conceptually similar to the

ISDN which BT is now installing. It is a weighty argument in favour of integrating BT's switched network with the cable companies' networks. BT would operate the trunk routes, using its optical fibre technology, while the cable companies would organise the local drops to each subscriber. This kind of mutual relation is known as interconnection. Total integration goes beyond the ITAP recommendations. The ITAP would prefer the private companies to construct local networks according to their own private corporate abilities, and for the national network to emerge piecemeal; to work from the bottom up rather than from the top down.

5.5.6. Several proposals have been made to build a coherent national network from the very beginnings. Whereas the cost of cabling half the country is estimated by the ITAP report to be about £2,500 million, the cost of a full national network has been put at £25,000 million, of which a substantial proportion will go to foreign companies, especially in the USA and Canada, which have many years experience in both cables and the associated electronics. The result would probably be the most advanced and thorough network of any industrialised country except perhaps the Bigfon network being planned for West Germany. However, the UK proposals are sketchy and unlikely to be given firm support.

5.5.7. There does seem widespread agreement both in North America and the UK that although the immediate attraction of more channels is entertainment (especially movies) the long term benefits will come from information services including transactions and remote control. The ITAP report acknowledges the 'paradox'. It says:

> We believe cable to be an essential component of future communications systems, offering great opportunities for new forms of entrepreneurial activity and substantial direct and indirect industrial benefits. However, the initial financing of cable systems will depend upon none of these things, but upon estimates of the revenue from additional popular programming channels. We consider the long term potential of cable systems for providing new sorts of services to be much more important, but have to accept that cable systems will go through an initial phase when their attraction will be based on 'entertainment' considerations. It is, though, essential that the technical specifications set for new cable systems should not preclude the transition from this initial phase to a subsequent phase when cable really does provide a full range of interactive services (para 8.5).

38

5.5.8. The Government has not formally responded to the I T A P report but the Home Secretary quoted the Prime Minister on 22 March when he spoke in the House of Commons in answer to a question about broadcasting policy. He said: 'The Government recognises the importance of the arguments in the I T A P Report and wishes to secure the benefits of this new technology for the U K'.

5.5.9. His main point was the need for more analysis of the implications. He therefore decided that, 'in parallel with the urgent studies which the Departments concerned will be carrying out into the economic, technical and telecommunications policy issues related to the expansion of cable, there should be an independent inquiry into the important broadcasting policy aspects.'

5.5.10. The committee which will carry out this inquiry is to be chaired by Lord Hunt (former Secretary to the Cabinet, 1973–9). Its other members are Maurice Hodgson (former Chairman, I C I) and Professor James Ring (Professor of Physics, Imperial College of Science and Technology and a former member of the I B A). The committee has now published a document detailing the questions of policy which it will consider. This document is given in full below.

5.5.11. INQUIRY INTO CABLE EXPANSION AND BROADCASTING POLICY

Consultation About The Issues Under Inquiry

The Inquiry has been asked by the Home Secretary:

> To take as its frame of reference the Government's wish to secure the benefits for the United Kingdom which cable technology can offer and its willingness to consider an expansion of cable systems which would permit cable to carry a wider range of entertainment and other services (including when available services of direct broadcasting by satellite), but in a way consistent with the wider public interest, in particular the safeguarding of public service broadcasting; to consider the questions affecting broadcasting policy which would arise from such an expansion, including in particular the supervisory framework; and to make recommendations by 30 September 1982.

The background is that so far governments in the United Kingdom have adopted the policy that broadcasting should be conducted only as a public service by public authorities set up for the purpose. The only authorities licensed to broadcast (the B B C and the I B A) are placed under an obligation to provide services for the dissemination of information, education and entertainment which maintain a high general standard both technically and in their content, a proper balance and a wide range in their subject matter. They also have specific obligations in relation to programme standards: to ensure so far as possible that nothing is included in their programmes which offends good taste and decency, is likely to encourage crime or lead to disorder, or to be offensive to public feeling; and that due impartiality is preserved in the presentation of news and in the treatment of controversial matters.

Hitherto the justification for this kind of regulation has rested on two features of broadcasting:

(a) it involves the use of a limited resource – transmitting frequencies – whose allocation is the subject of international negotiation between governments;

(b) it is a powerful medium which is brought direct into people's homes, with great potential to influence or offend them there.

The part played by cable systems to date has fitted into this framework in that the essential function of the systems has been to relay BBC and ITV (and independent local radio) programmes. The extension of the provision of other programme services by cable systems would bypass the shortage of radio frequencies and the main need for regulation described above would not therefore arise. Furthermore, if cable systems are to be developed for additional services, there are economic and other arguments for giving the maximum incentive by providing a wide choice of programmes as quickly as possible. Indeed, one view is that broadcasting by cable should be regarded simply as another branch of publishing, with no more control or restriction than applies to the written press – for example, the restrictions on such matters as defamation, sedition and obscenity which are imposed by law. If this view is accepted, there is no need for regulation at all, though a voluntary code, possibly monitored by a body like the Press Council, would not be ruled out.

On the other hand it can be argued that the expansion of cable services would not remove all need for some degree of regulation. Broadly these arguments are that:

(a) cable is different from the written press, not only because there is almost bound to be an effective monopoly in any given local area, but also because a large part of the country will continue to depend on off-air services for the foreseeable future;

(b) an expansion of programme services by cable could damage the quality and range of public service broadcasting, on which viewers who cannot receive or do not wish to pay for cable services would continue to depend, by obtaining exclusive rights to national and sporting events, etc., or by attracting audiences (and in the case of ITV advertising revenue) away from broadcast services and leaving them less able to provide the range of programmes now offered;

(c) regardless of the medium of transmission, television programmes brought direct into the home have a power, an intimacy and an influence which justifies supervision.

These questions relating to whether there is a need for regulation are central to the Inquiry's task, and it would welcome views and comments on the way in which the question of regulation should be approached and on the supervisory framework (if any) which might be appropriate.

Within this general question, a number of more particular issues arise on which the Inquiry would like to have views. Among these are:

1. Should there be restrictions on the scale or ownership of cable companies, e.g., to prevent excessive monopoly or to exclude or limit foreign interests, political or religious groups, the press or existing broadcasters?

2. Should there be separation between the cable operator and the programme provider, in order to facilitate a multiplicity of programme providers on each cable system? This arrangement would also make it easier, in cases of unsatisfactory performance, to exclude a programme provider without robbing the cable customer of all home entertainment services. Or is the incentive to cable and the demand for connection so closely related to the programmes to be provided that the cable operator cannot realistically be asked to forgo the opportunity to provide programmes?

3. What should be the basis of finance of cable entertainment? Should it be subscription, or should cable companies be permitted to finance themselves wholly or partly from advertising? If advertising were to be allowed should it be subject to control and supervision (cf. the IBA system)? What repercussions would follow for independent television, independent local radio or local newspapers?

4. Should the present obligation on cable operators to relay the broadcast services of the BBC and IBA be retained? Or is there a case for removing it altogether or modifying it or waiving it for a limited period (the last course being intended to allow cable operators to maximise revenue from their existing limited capacity cable until they can lay down wideband cable which will have adequate capacity for broadcast services along with others)?

5. Should cable operators be under an obligation (as the broadcasting authorities are) to provide a wide range and balance of programmes, including programmes for minority interests? If so, would it be reasonable for the obligation to apply to the totality of programme channels on a cable system rather than to each channel individually?

6. Should the traditional broadcasting requirements relating to taste and decency and the suitability of programmes for children likely to be watching be imposed on cable services? If certain channels can be received only by payment of an additional fee should the operator be free to supply on those channels programmes which might offend others, subject only to the application of criminal law? Is there scope for specific rules related to the censorship category of cinema films (as in the subscription television pilot schemes, which preclude 'X' films being shown before 10 p.m.)?

7. Should the traditional broadcasting requirements relating to impartiality be imposed on cable services, or should it be possible for particular interest groups to provide programmes or even to run individual channels?

8. Should there be formal safeguards against cable systems obtaining exclusive rights to certain events (along the lines of those in section 30 of the Broadcasting Act 1981 restricting exclusivity by one of the broadcasting authorities) or otherwise intended to prevent the impoverishment of broadcast services?

9. Should there be any restriction on the relay of foreign broadcasting services or on the proportion of foreign programme material included in cable services?

10. Should there be any protection for the cinema industry through a restriction on the showing on cable television of new films? (Films are not normally shown on television until they are three years old; and the licence for the sub-

scription television pilot schemes precludes the showing of films within twelve months of their being first registered.)

11. If there were to be a need for a supervisory framework other than self-regulation, what should be the means of supervision? Is there scope for local supervision, or should it be carried out by some national body? Could the responsibility appropriately be given to an existing body or is a new public body needed?

12. What powers and sanctions would be necessary or desirable to ensure compliance with any scheme of regulation which might be adopted?

These questions are not intended to limit the scope of the representations which the Inquiry is inviting, but merely to help to direct comments towards the issues which the Inquiry thinks it will need to resolve. General views and constructive proposals on these and any matters within the Inquiry's terms of reference should be sent to the Secretary to the Inquiry at the address below as soon as possible. It would be helpful to the Inquiry to know in the meantime which of the bodies receiving this invitation proposes to submit evidence, which should be received preferably by 31 May 1982 at the latest.

> J. C. DAVEY,
> *Inquiry into Cable Expansion and Broadcasting Policy,*
> Whittington House,
> 19–30 Alfred Place,
> London WC1 7EJ.

5.5.12. The 'urgent studies' mentioned by William Whitelaw are co-ordinated by the Cabinet Office IT Unit and are interdepartmental. They are:

1. *Technological and Commercial Aspects*
Chaired by Industry, with membership initially of Industry, Home Office, Cabinet Office and Trade. The leading issue is the question of switched or tree-type systems.

2. *Telecommunications Structure*
Chaired by Industry, with membership of Industry, Home Office, Cabinet Office, Treasury, Trade, Environment/Transport. The role of British Telecom.

3. *Economic Aspects*
Chaired by Treasury. Members include Industry, Home Office, Cabinet Office, Trade and Employment. Includes the relationship between cable and film, Fleet Street and the local press; and employment implications.

4. *Broadcasting*
Chaired by Home Office. Members include Industry, Cabinet Office, Treasury and Trade. This committee will look at the relationship between broadcasting and telecommunications.

5.5.13. There has been little public discussion of the developments so far or of the future possibilities. But Brian Wenham, Controller, B B C-2, has suggested (*The Observer*, 21 March):

> From the narrow point of view of 'citizen as viewer' one fact already looms large: the new technology will spread patchily, and with no necessary guarantee that it will ever be available to all. In other words we are dealing with additional facility, not with public utility. This is in sharp contrast with the network broadcasting of B B C-1, B B C-2, I T V-1 and also Channel Four.
>
> In a nutshell, the interest of the 'citizen as viewer' requires that until such time as the new technologies are made available to all expansion of television services should be arranged and guided so as not to deprive the network-viewer of what he or she now receives. That means not only that the cable-viewer should automatically receive the basic networks as part of his or her cable package, but also that the non-cable viewer should continue to receive a mix of programmes of similar quality to those currently broadcast. The difficulty here, of course, is that it may well be that the easiest way forward for the *new* television services would be to plunder the proven successes and attractions of the *old*.
>
> Were you to take a poll of television's top 200 executives, you find that most expect the first battleground to be provided by sport. New information technologies that could in theory leapfrog economic divisions and provide a new level starting point for all may, in the event, be led in a quite opposite direction. Were this to be the case then there would be an open need for vigilance on behalf of the general viewer, to ensure that he is not gradually and persistently disenfranchised by stealth. Such vigilance should not be the province of broadcasters alone.

5.5.14. Pay- T V and every other form of transactional television, either the current forms of pay per channel or the future alternative of pay per programme, has implications for the film industry, especially the exhibitors. The Cinematograph Films Council has given a cautious welcome to pay- T V as a stimulus to film production, but it fears the challenge to the cinema exhibitors. The Council's position was summarised in its 43rd Annual Report for 1980/1:

> I. Council is conscious that it is unable at this time to provide a detailed solution for all the problems of a newly commissioned S T V [i.e. pay- T V] service. However, it believes that an attempt must be made to formulate policies promptly, otherwise British interests will be handicapped by indecision and will be overtaken by foreign competition.

II. Council welcomes the development of STV which it sees as a stimulus to film and other theatrical production, to which it hopes the STV companies will become financial contributors; but there will need to be certain safeguards imposed.

III. It is felt that local cinema exhibitors should always be given the opportunity to be involved in pilot schemes, so that appropriate attention can be given to local problems and preferences. There should be a specific period during which newly released films are reserved for cinema exhibition before being released to STV. Films which have been certified by the British Board of Film Censors as suitable for exhibition to adults should only be shown in the late evening.

IV. In order to encourage the production of short films there should be no discrimination against the screening of filmed material which is less than an hour in length, providing that material was originally registered as a cinema film.

V. As long as cinemas are so regulated (the screen quota), there should be a similar requirement to screen a prescribed proportion of British or Community films amongst those shown.

VI. Council further expects that a levy will be charged on the screening of films which have been registered for cinema exhibition (similar to the Eady levy on the receipts of cinema exhibitors) and that this will be directed to the benefit of the cinema film industry.

5.5.15. It is not surprising that the CFC was 'unable to provide a detailed solution to all the problems' of pay-TV. Such an overweening ambition is uncharacteristic of the Council, which has a better reputation for discussion about the industry's existing problems than for making moves towards the innovation of future services. Its recommendation that local cinema exhibitors should be involved was in line with several other proposals (e.g. Sir Harold Wilson's parliamentary questions on 15 December 1980) that the pay-TV licences should not be limited to the existing cable operators; but it was rejected. Equally important were its proposals on quota and levy; but these quintessentially film matters found no favour in the Home Office's Broadcasting Department; perhaps, quite properly during the period of the experiment, they were felt to be premature and administratively burdensome.

5.5.16. The proposal for a levy on 'new media' was made by the Interim Action Committee on the Film Industry in its Fifth Report, *The Distribution of Films for Exhibition in Cinemas and by Other Means* (March 1982). The report said that 'The exhibition or sale of feature films through the media must carry with it a contribution to the Eady levy' (paragraph 89).

6 Interactive and Textual Systems

6.1. Several new systems provide a degree of interaction between a user/viewer and the source of a signal, via a TV set. 'Interaction' is a much abused word; it properly implies a two-way communications system in which each communications channel is equidistant. The capacities of the send and return channels can be very different. While a face-to-face conversation is said to be really interactive only if the two people take an equal part, a communication system is said to be interactive if one channel is video and the return channel only data.

6.2.1. The simplest systems are broadcast videotex, or teletext, which have been developed by broadcasting organisations, and have been conceived as one-way systems in the traditional mould of one-way broadcasting. The viewer's interaction is limited to selecting one of a number of pages (screenfuls) of text and graphics that are transmitted as part of the ordinary TV signal. The information is encoded in four 'spare' lines of the 625-line picture. All teletext services are provided without charge, partly because the broadcasting organisation has no way of knowing who is using which pages.

6.2.2. A variant of a basic teletext service is now being provided in about two dozen countries on an operational or experimental basis. Technically the systems are very similar, and most are compatible because they are derived from the BBC's Ceefax which, with the IBA's Oracle, was the world's first system.

6.2.3. The first Ceefax trials started in 1974 and Ceefax and Oracle went public in 1978. Ceefax now provides about 100 pages on BBC-1 and 100 pages on BBC-2, covering news headlines, sports results, travel, weather information, traffic news, the TV schedules, etc. Oracle has slightly more pages but the overall mix is similar. Some CIT research in October 1981 suggests that on average teletext was used 1.4 times a day with an average of 4.7 pages being read each time. Peak usage was at 6 p.m. Both Ceefax and Oracle are national services but Oracle, starting with Scotland, is increasing its regional opt-outs. Oracle is also selling full-page and crawl advertisements. The ads are regulated by the IBA according to a slightly different code of practice from the code covering ITV's regular broadcasts.

46

6.2.4. The UK's teletext services have been more successful than Prestel, if less well publicised. At the end of 1981 the UK had 300,000 sets capable of receiving the two services, and by Spring 1982 deliveries to shops were running at 40,000 per month. The extra price of £100 per set is now more generally acceptable and many so-called 'replacement' sets (replacing colour sets bought in the boom of the early 1970s) have a teletext facility. The main problem remains, however, that in any teletext service either the number of pages per channel is limited to about 100/200 or the waiting-time for a page is unacceptable. At present, an ordinary user may have to wait 20/30 seconds for a page, which discourages people from using it. Skilled users can cut down on the waiting time, but not by much. This timing constraint could disappear if teletext was allowed to use an entire channel, with its 625 lines, instead of the maximum of four or six lines as at present. The French are considering such a plan, and there are hints of a UK teletext channel in the Home Office's recent report on satellites. The VHF channels could also be re-engineered for teletext.

6.3.1. The next level of system has been developed by national telecommunication authorities as a means of exploiting the telephone system. They are called wired videotex or viewdata systems. The viewer uses the public switched 'telephone' network to transmit requests for pages to a central data bank which then sends back the appropriate page. The discrete interactivity of the system allows the organisations to make a charge each time it is used.

6.3.2. The pioneers of this kind of wired videotex are the UK, France and Canada. The UK and France developed the first generation of wired videotex systems, called respectively Prestel and Télétel; the Canadians developed an improved second generation, called Telidon, and AT&T, the giant US telephone company, has adopted a version of Telidon for use in the USA.

6.3.3. Each information provider to Prestel must pay an annual registration fee of £5,000, and a further £5 per page per year. However, it is possible to use an existing information provider (known as an 'umbrella' IP) to process one's pages; in this case one avoids the £5,000 entry fee. These costs, of course, are only a minor part of the operation. The major cost is the preparation and design of the page itself. According to Mills & Allen, a major 'umbrella' IP, the average cost of a page is £55 per year.

6.3.4. Most information providers recoup some of the costs of supplying information to Prestel by charging users for accessing their pages. The current per page charges vary from one p. to 50p.; the median is probably 5–10p. However, many information providers make no charge. One snag about Prestel's charging system is that the user may not know until he is actually using a page whether or not it is free.

6.3.5. It is possible to use Prestel and similar systems to provide a range of fairly specific communications between the information provider and the user. The user automatically registers whether he/she is using a page (necessary for billing). He/she can also indicate preferences by selecting between a range of alternatives; in some circumstances, such selection could constitute voting. It is also possible to use a personal code number (e.g. of a credit card) to purchase goods.

6.3.6. Whereas Ceefax and Oracle have always been seen as an integral part of mass broadcasting, Prestel, after some over-optimistic talk of the 'wired nation', is now aimed almost exclusively at business and industry. But at the end of 1981 only a meagre 15,000 Prestel TV sets were in use. There were four main categories of users: the TV industry (2,000 sets); residential (2,500 sets), of which at least half were really business sets; travel (2,500 sets); and general business (8,000 sets). The Prestel directorate spent 1981 in retrenchment: computers were closed and some staff made redundant. In 1982 several new policies may effect radical change. The Prestel directorate may become more actively a partner with IPs (it may decide to vet IP pages, which would end the cherished notion of Prestel as a common carrier). It has already given tremendous encouragement to the idea of Private Prestel (or closed user groups), in which organisations use Prestel either to distribute information to a restricted group of subscribers or to distribute special information which may be kept in the organisation's own data bank. In this sense, Prestel provides a gateway to the IPs' own resources. Early in 1982 Prestel reduced the Private Prestel tariff for closed user groups from £2,500 to £250 and increased from 50 to 32,000 the number of closed user groups that Prestel could accommodate. Private Prestel services are likely to be a major growth area during the next few years, further changing the original idea.

6.3.7. The move towards Prestel as 'gateway' recognises both the enormous potential of wired videotex and Prestel's failure to exploit it. The ITAP report says firmly that 'virtually all the extra services now being promoted on American cable systems are in fact based on viewdata or teletext principles' (i.e. videotex). It is also clear from Qube and other advanced systems that the major attraction of wired videotex is its transactional service. People like to use the TV set. They like to play with it. They like to reach out to get information and advice. A 1981 report by the US IRD consultancy company talked of US revenues of $1,500 million in 1991 not only in cable security, control and alarms systems but also in transactional services, excluding the values of the transactions themselves. Banking-at-home, shopping-at-home and 'Seek and Find' (e.g. scanning classified ads and making a purchase) were suggested as major attractions. The IRD report's conclusions, supported by Qube management, was that 'information without the possibility of a transaction will eventually become unexciting.'

6.4.1. A third level of system has been developed in the USA and Canada by private companies and in Japan by a consortium of government ministries. These systems are neither extensions of the traditional broadcasting service nor of the telephone system. They are much more ambitious, and offer a whole scale of different services, ranging from special entertainment programmes that can be specially ordered (and paid for) to sensing devices for the monitoring of heating and lighting.

6.4.2. The most notable are Warner's Qube, which opened in Columbus, Ohio, and is now being installed in five US cities, and the HI-Ovis experiments in several Japanese towns. These systems provide a hierarchy of conventional TV/sound programmes, premium pay-TV, special services of repeats, 'still' pictures, community programmes, etc., and additional security services to control lighting and heating and to protect against fire and burglary. The Japanese experiments are very costly, and there seems little chance of further systems being installed on an economic basis. The Qube systems are more successful, although Warner Amex is far from recouping its investment.

6.4.3. These imaginative interactive systems were mentioned in the ITAP report as desirable devices for the future, but their provision and function seems vague. British Telecom has a 21-household network at Milton Keynes, equipped with an interesting variety of two-way services, but the experience so far offers little guidance.

6.4.4. Granada TV and Channel Four are also experimenting with interactive sevices. Granada is equipping over 100 households in Manchester and Liverpool with keyboards and terminals that will allow users to register likes and dislikes about ITV programmes. Channel Four is doing much the same with 100 households in London. Both experiments are being monitored by AGB Cable and Viewdata, with equipment supplied by Philips. The results will be processed through a Prestel gateway.

6.4.5. For all interactive systems the term 'viewer' implies someone too passive, too much a subject of a process being controlled elsewhere. It is better to speak of 'users'. It is better to think of people who sometimes use the TV set (and other gadgets) to get hold of and display information: the news, a film, or the sports results. It is best to see the T V set as the entry and exit of a multiplicity of networks.

7 Storage: Cassettes and Discs

7.1. As the number of TV channels increases, both over-the-air and by cable, so our ability to record, store and replay material where and when we want is also increasing. Of course, there is a mutual complementarity in the two trends; the increase in the number of channels makes it more desirable that people should have some means of scheduling and arranging the material they want to use and, in turn, that ability makes them able to cope with the larger number of channels. These storage devices symbolise the new independence of the TV user.

CASSETTES

7.2.1. The video cassette is now firmly established as a highly desirable partner to the TV set. After the shaky start of Philips' VCR in the early seventies the new models' sales and rentals have regularly outdistanced predictions. In the USA some 800,000 cassette machines were sold in 1980 and 1,360,000 were sold in 1981, making a total of 2,750,000 (about 4% of TV households). In the UK, about 400,000 were sold in 1980 and about 1,000,000 in 1981 (totalling about 6% of TV households). The average of most estimates for 1985 produces a total UK population of about five million (25% of homes). Already, in the UK, the trade in cassette players (£550 million) represents a greater annual retail turnover than both radio sets and hi-fi sets; and it is catching up with the turnover in TV sets (£650 million).

7.2.2. There are three dominant formats, each representing a second generation system. The Japan Victor Company's VHS system, helped by the support of the powerful rental companies, is by far the most popular, with about 60% of the market. The second major system is based on the Sony Beta format. These two Japanese formats are basically similar. The Philips V2000 series, introduced in 1979 with a flip-over cassette providing eight hours playing time, is fundamentally different. The Philips and related Grundig machines are superior to the Japanese models in some respects but have entered the market too late to have captured more than a 10% share. No new systems are imminent. However, new tape formats are being developed which are cheaper and can provide longer playing times, so the cost of an hour's recording is constantly falling.

7.2.3. In the UK, though not so much elsewhere, cassettes are used mostly for time-shift recording and are already affecting the ways in which people regard both their TV sets and the broadcasters' TV programmes. Estimates for the amount of time-shifted recordings that are actually watched range from 75% down to 25%; the figures are low in the context of people's traditional attitude to TV but high in comparison with magazines, newspapers, books, etc. Cassette owners tend to be active users rather than passive viewers. They tend to be more selective in tailoring their viewing to their own wants. The result may be a decline in overall viewing as the cassette owner stops watching the 'least worst' of what's on and begins to watch only those things that he really wants to watch. On the other hand the purchase (or rent) of pre-recorded cassettes may increase time-shifting and overall viewing as people try to find time to watch the extra material.

7.2.4. There is a small but active trade in pre-recorded cassettes. The most popular subjects are films, sports, music and sex. The market is small because pre-recorded cassettes are expensive (up to a top of about £40, and £3 to rent); especially when compared to the 'free' material being transmitted in such quantities by the broadcasting organisations. But the market is growing. The future scope of the pre-recorded cassette market depends very much on the developments in video discs.

7.2.5. The use of cassettes to record off-air raises the question of copyright in an especially awkward form. This note can give only a summary. The basic UK law is the 1956 Copyright Act, which was enacted long before video cassettes were invented, and is acknowledged to need urgent reform. A thorough review of all UK copyright matters was made by the Whitford Committee which reported (unfortunately, not always unanimously) in 1977. The government accepted a few of Whitford's recommendations, but the lack of unanimity prevented any basic change. The next step was the publication of a consultative Green Paper, *Reform of the Law relating to Copyright, Designs and Performers' Protection,* in 1981, with a request for comments. The Department of Trade, through its Industrial Property and Copyright Department, is now studying these responses.

7.2.6. Several specific problems may be mentioned. The first problem is the legality or not of recording off-air any material for which copyright has not been properly assigned and paid or intended to be paid. Copyright owners can seek redress under civil law or criminal law. Both courses are unsatisfactory. Under civil law, the copyright owner can seek an injunction (often involving an 'Anton Piller' order for collecting evidence). The procedure is not really appropriate. Under criminal law, charges can result in a maximum £50 fine, which is not enough to deter serious offenders. In exceptional instances the police may bring a charge of 'conspiracy to defraud' but such cases are burdensome and expensive, and convictions are rare. So far, prosecutions have been limited to instances where the recording and/or playback have taken place in public places (often involving pre-recorded cassettes). There have been no prosecutions of individuals recording at home and replaying at home.

7.2.7. An especially contentious area is the performance of a cassette in a public place. Already, many people are buying or renting pre-recorded cassettes, or recording off-air, and playing them in various places (pubs, clubs) to a public audience. Many people do not know that such performance is, in most cases, against the law. To get permission for such performances from the copyright owner is usually impossible because it involves complex negotiations for a tiny return. There are several proposals to establish a 'blanket' licence scheme by which places could be licensed for such performances in return for a copyright levy whose proceeds would be paid to the copyright owners.

7.2.8. The Whitford Committee proposed a levy on the sale price of each video cassette player. But the Green Paper argued that most people use their players not to watch material that they otherwise would not watch but rather to watch material at a different (more convenient) time; therefore, the copyright owner's commercial interests were not detrimentally affected; therefore no levy, either on equipment or on blank tape. Most UK copyright owners, the BBC and ITCA and the world record industry, however, are lobbying strongly for a levy on blank tape and/or equipment. An alternative method for stopping illegal recording is to ensure that every tape incorporates a spoiler device to make re-recording technically impossible.

7.2.9. Rental poses another problem. The Copyright Act protects the copyright owner against unlawful copying, performance, broadcasting and diffusion (i.e. wired transmission). But it provides no protection against misuse during rental. The relevant law for rental is not copyright at all but the entirely different contract law or law of tort, for which the copyright owner or rental operator has to devise quite complex contracts for each case. There are various proposals to bring rental within the area of copyright proper.

7.2.10. It would probably be wrong to take the US experience as a guide, except in the one essential matter: that legislators fight shy of copyright reform. The latest development, after five years of hearings, is that the Ninth Court of Appeals in San Francisco has ruled that it is illegal to record TV programmes off a TV set on to videotape or

53

cassettes. The court was ruling on a case brought by Universal Studios and Walt Disney Productions against the Sony Corporation (and others). Its decision overturns a 1979 ruling by a lower court that off-air recording was permissible. The defendants have appealed to the Supreme Court. At the moment the situation can be described mildly as total confusion.

7.2.11. The 1971 Copyright Act exempted the home taping of audio programmes, and the lower court depended on that precedent for its ruling that video taping was also legal. But the San Francisco Court of Appeals disagreed. It said that in 1971 Congress had been unaware of the possibility of home video recording and that their provisions could not be held to apply to it. Therefore, home video copying, for whatever purpose, was liable to copyright restrictions. Nobody expects to be able to collect copyright payments from individual people. By common consent the most likely compromise is for a levy on blank tapes. But that discriminates unfairly against those who buy tapes for other reasons (e.g. professional uses, or where copyright is paid directly).

7.2.12. The matter may be resolved by Congressional reform of the copyright laws. Senator de Concini has proposed a 'blanket exemption' while Senator Mathias would establish a system of surcharges (levies) and compulsory licensing. The Mathias amendment has been strongly supported by the Motion Picture Association of America. But it faces opposition from both senators and representatives who prefer a simple 'blanket' exemption and who don't want to get involved in copyright matters.

VIDEO DISCS

7.3.1. The disc has been a storage device for information of all kinds for a long time, as witnessed by gramophone records, the floppy discs used for computerised data memories and the twin-headed discs used by TV stations for 'action replays' and slow motion. But the development of the disc for home video has been plagued by trouble. The grand ambitions of the early 1970s have not been fulfilled. As a means of storing and providing instant access to each separate bit of information the disc is manifestly better than a reel of tape. These qualities are enough to make it highly desirable for industry, retailing, libraries, research, etc. But the disc has an endemic weakness. The professional systems are expensive and inflexible. And the cheaper, simpler home systems cannot record on their own discs. Any success of the disc as an industrial, professional tool (and the USA can tell some remarkable success stories) is therefore irrelevant to the immediate success of the video disc in the home.

54

7.3.2. The consumer disc does have some advantages compared to the cassette, however. It is cheaper and easier to handle. It is even easier to play a video disc than an audio disc, because the video disc player is more automated. So what's the problem? The great advantage of the disc is its source of a cheap supply of film and television. Its great disadvantage is that it cannot record off-air, and must therefore rely on pre-recorded discs. The drawback is considerable, because it raises, without any hope of escape, the problem of the chicken and the egg which bedevils every new medium to varying degrees. Which comes first: the gadgets or the programmes? The first disc failed because nobody wanted to watch its programmes. Laservision and Selectavision players are sticking badly because their programmes are unappealing. The industry hopes that the weight of the entertainment conglomerates that are now beginning to back discs (including the three US networks, MCA, Philips, Polygram, Beta, 20th Century-Fox, Universal, Rank and EMI) will tip the balance; in other words, that enough attractive discs will be produced for enough discs to be sold, and so on, snowballing towards the huge profits that are forecast for the disc by the end of the 1980s. But when, or if, that critical point will be reached is anyone's guess.

7.3.3. The high visibility of the disc stems from this awareness among film companies, entertainment conglomerates and investment houses that the video disc allows any independent company to make and sell television. To sell television directly into people's homes.

7.3.4. The first video disc system was the Tel-Dec, developed by Telefunken and Decca in the early 1970s. It was a flop, because the discs were only ten minutes long and the programmes were banal. It was several years before Tel-Dec and its contemporaries were finally put to rest and manufacturers started to generate the second generation disc systems. The leading proponents were Philips, Matsushita and RCA; Sony, which had pioneered video cassettes, decided that discs were a loser, and recent events have confirmed the company in its scepticism.

7.3.5. The first of the new systems was Philips' Laservision (originally Discovision) which Philips' subsidiary Magnavox launched in the USA at Christmas 1978. Laservision was the first optical disc system. It works by focusing a laser on a series of pits on the disc's surface. Two models have been developed. The more primitive has a constant rotational speed of 1,500 rpm and produces 30 minutes of playing time each side. A later development uses variable rotational speed, but a constant tangential velocity, to produce 60 minutes a side (with a constant tangential velocity the disc slows from 1,500 rpm to 500 rpm as the laser beam moves outwards). In the three years since being launched, after two years of regional test marketing and one year of national sales, Laservision has sold 75,000 players, at a list price of $750.

7.3.6. Laservision has been prepared three times for a UK launch. The latest attempt was May 1982. But production problems at the Blackburn, Lancashire, disc factory, and other marketing difficulties have compelled the company to cancel. Philips also have distribution problems. Granada Television Rental has continually said it will not handle Laservision, and Thorn-EMI's Radio Rentals is committed to selling only its parent's rival VHD system. Philips also had some problems in the USA when IBM and MCA decided to sell their shares in Discovision Associates to the Pioneer (Japan) company. The history of videodiscs is full of quick marriages and tangled divorces. The results for Philips are that Laservision, if launched as now planned in September 1982, will only be available in London and the South-East and only with 75 titles. The price, too, is expensive. The players are likely to cost £500 and the discs around £17.

7.3.7. The only other disc system now available is RCA's Selectavision (also called CED, or capacitance electronic disc). Selectavision uses the more conventional technology of a stylus in a groove which makes it cheaper than Laservision and other optical systems, although it cannot provide some of the optical system's more fancy options of freeze frame or slow scan. The disc rotates at 450 rpm. Selectavision was launched in the USA in March 1981. RCA hoped to sell 200,000 players in its first year at a list price of $500; it actually sold only 65,000. As a result of these low sales RCA's disc division has reported losses of $106 million in 1981 (with R & D costs of $21 million in 1979 and $56 million in 1980). In Spring 1982 RCA cut the list price of a player to $300. As with Laservision the range of discs is very small. The 1982 Sears Spring catalogue lists only 52 titles, Montgomery Ward only 20 and J. C. Penney only 64. RCA's own research indicates that the average Selectavision user bought as many as 18 discs in the first year (a considerable expenditure) so if interest and income is to be maintained the number of titles will have to be increased. RCA's plans to sell Selectavision in the UK have not been confirmed but it is unlikely to be available before 1983, and could well be delayed for some time. Selectavision players are cheaper than Laservision, with a probable UK price of £300, but the discs will cost the same at about £15.

7.3.8. The third major system has been developed by the Japanese Victor Company (JVC), the same Matsushita subsidiary that developed the best selling VHS video cassette system. The JVC disc system is called

VHD (video high density) in its video mode and AHD (audio high density) in its audio mode. Like Selectavision it uses a traditional stylus and groove. VHD is not yet available, anywhere. JVC's scheduled launch in Japan was postponed because of the country's 'sluggish economy' and the US failure of Laservision and Selectavision. The USA launch, planned by General Electric for Autumn 1982, is thus in jeopardy. The UK launch, by Thorn-EMI, was to have been September but it may now be postponed and the trade would not be surprised if VHD did not appear this year. In price VHD is expected to be midway between Laservision and Selectavision.

8 Display

8.1. Most of these devices centre on the TV set. Today's TV set is obviously the box in the corner and today's TV is what we watch on the box. Tomorrow, there will be several boxes, some of which will have screens, and some not, and the screens will show a Hollywood movie, a home movie and a list of local restaurants with equal facility.

8.2. As today one can buy a radio receiver in many forms varying from a cheap transistor to a much more powerful multi-unit system, so we will be able to buy television sets of all shapes and sizes. Screen diameters will vary from a few inches up to six feet. Portable sets will become more common, and many sets will be viewed outside the main living-room and often in bad lighting conditions. Remote control will become very common (helped by the spread of teletext and video cassette players) although the introduction of sets sensitive to spoken commands, as demonstrated by Mitsubishi at several trade shows in 1981, is some way from economic production. Many manufacturers (notably Bang & Olufsen, Philips, Sony) are now putting greater efforts behind improving the quality of sound. Most TV sets have cheap loudspeakers, absolutely incapable of reproducing the high quality sound transmitted by the broadcasting organisations and incapable, too, of reproducing the quality of sound pre-recorded on a video disc or cassette. The next step, perhaps, is stereo sound (easily provided by a satellite's SHF wave-bands). Already some terrestrial transmitters in West Germany and Sweden are providing a degree of stereo sound. In the USA, the FCC has decided to let the marketplace decide its preference amongst five incompatible stereo systems.

8.3. There are four main areas of development. Since the TV manufacturing industry is a worldwide business each development is being pursued across a broad front, and final product design and standardisation may await global agreement. Some manufacturers, notably the large Japanese corporations, regard standardisation as a secondary matter after the top priority of designing the best possible product. The four areas of interest are: high definition television; 3-D; very large screens; and flat screens. Some of these innovations require only new receivers. But in all cases, the new investment is very substantial, and sudden change on a massive scale is improbable.

8.4.1. The advent of high-definition television (HDTV) is potentially one of the most exciting and significant developments of the next few years. The pictorial improvement is very substantial. The Chairman of the EBU Technical Committee has reported that the difference between the US experiments in 1125-line displays and the existing NTSC 525 system is greater than the difference between colour and black-and-white. The uses of HDTV in video production, in broadcast television and in large-screen cinematic display will deeply affect the TV and film industries, forever changing their patterns of production, distribution and display. Industry crossovers, particularly transferring from HDTV tape to 35 mm film, will blur industry boundaries even more.

8.4.2. The most advanced HDTV system is the 1125-line standard invented by NHK, the Japan Broadcasting Corporation, and promoted by CBS in the USA (with some help from Télédiffusion de France). The NHK/CBS system not only uses more than twice the US standard number of lines but also a different aspect ratio. CBS held its first over-the-air transmission tests in March 1982, using the 12 GHz allocated worldwide for satellite services.

8.4.3. Of all new technologies, high-definition television is the most abstruse and arguable. The issue is not really high but higher definition television: the improvement of signals and coding to provide a better, clearer, more vivid picture. Existing picture standards can be improved in many ways. Higher resolution, although dramatic, is only one of many possibilities; the others include different aspect ratios, wider bandwidth, different treatment of the separate luminance and chrominance (colour signals) and many more. Both the BBC and IBA are working on ways of improving their network transmissions by these means. The BBC is thinking of using a separate frequency to transmit a parallel signal that would be integrated with the main signal for display. The IBA has developed a multiplex analogue component (MAC) which would separate the signals by time, not by frequency. A key element in both plans is the problem of HDTV's compatibility with existing equipment.

8.4.4. The advent of higher resolution services depends very much on political judgements about the need to protect the public's investments in the existing systems of 525, 625, etc. lines. There are also schemes for studio recording with a high resolution for cassette, disc (cable?) distribution but for continuing to transmit over-the-air at the existing 625 lines, although it might be possible for a special unit at the home TV set to recapture some of the recorded quality.

8.5.1. Several 3-D TV programmes have been broadcast recently in Europe and the USA. The programmes have been made with slightly different systems, but the basic principle of the anaglyph system that first appeared in the 1930s is still the most popular. The crude system requires spectacles and produces a black-and-white picture (or a red-and-green picture). In West Germany the ARD third network has shown NDR's two-part special and the Dutch NOS has collaborated with Philips to produce a two-hour special. Extracts from both countries' efforts were shown in the UK by TVS, a regional ITV company, on *The Real World* (4 May 1982). Over 500,000 cellophane spectacles were distributed in the South and South-East.

8.5.2. All the systems depend upon the viewer wearing spectacles. The anaglyph spectacles have a red filter in the left eye and a green filter in the right eye. The viewer sees a proper 3-D picture, but the colours are artificial. There is another problem: viewers without spectacles see only a blur. Several alternative systems have been developed, and more are promised. But nobody seems close to developing a 3-D system that has the minimum attributes of producing an ordinary colour picture for people without spectacles and a 3-D colour picture for people with spectacles. The development of 'direction-sensitive' screens is the next step. They don't depend on spectacles, but they have other drawbacks; for instance the viewer cannot move around the room without losing the 3-D effect. The success of 3-D requires a system that is fully compatible and can be viewed by a person who doesn't need spectacles and doesn't need to keep still. Until then, it remains a slight curiosity.

8.6.1. The invention of front projection has allowed video signals to be displayed on very large screens. There have also been some trials of back projection. The trouble with front projection so far has been that the picture has to be projected from a single large tube or sometimes three tubes about six feet in front of the screen. The technology is awkward and expensive, and the pictures are often rather hazy and dim (with the horizontal lines becoming visible). Front projection is likely to be restricted to public and group showings, probably linked to cassettes and discs. The better alternative of back screen projection is now being demonstrated in the USA, and has greater prospects, but the sets are likely to remain expensive.

8.6.2. EMI Cinemas have opened video cinemas in Purley, Basildon, Warrington, Huddersfield, Southampton, Waltham Cross and Cirencester. All cinemas except one have used a pair of Sony $\frac{3}{4}$ inch U-Matic cassette players and a Sony VPP 720 front screen projector. The cinemas typically have six rows each of twelve seats facing a screen 10 feet wide. The ACTT Technical Committee has criticised the screen as being too large and have said that since the quality falls short of the conventional 35mm standard, the public should be (*a*) informed in advance of the means of projection and (*b*) charged less than for a conventional cinema.

8.7. Flat screens are some way in the future. They require a new method of display to replace the cathode ray tube. A matrix of Charge Coupled Devices (CCDs) is the most likely contender and is already used in some specialist systems. But modern CCDs cannot compare in quality with the cathode ray tube. It is possible, however, that manufacturers will be unwilling to develop HDTV systems unless a flat screen digital display can be incorporated simultaneously.

8.8. All four innovations are likely to be combined at least in the design stage and for the setting of global standards. The huge investment in equipment, by operators and users, militates against the manufacturing of sets that can cope with one innovation but not with others that may be developed in subsequent years. But the current interest in HDTV has made both industry and users very aware that the conventional TV set is a relatively old-fashioned piece of video equipment, with considerable scope for improvement.

9 The Regulation of Information and Communications

9.1. The manner of regulation of broadcasting, video and film has become more contentious as new technologies and new social needs and wants make the traditional structures seem to be inequitable and contradictory. Too many organisations are forced to be defensive; too few policies are imaginative and flexible enough to be innovative. Most organisations analyse new technologies to see if they might challenge existing bureaucratic standards. Very few ask if new technologies can satisfy new social needs. In common with most European countries the UK has never formulated a coherent policy towards its information and communication activities. The BBC, Fleet Street and the public lending library were never subsumed under the heading of 'communications industry' until they started to buy the same microelectric equipment. This innocence is in danger of becoming naivety. The hallmark of the information society is that policies on information and communication become a chief element in the national interest.

9.2. Information Technology Year 82 is the symbol of this new awareness. It has three elements: the industrial imperative; the government's assignment of ministerial responsibilities; and the possible role of users in the monitoring and assessment of policy and the formulation of new policy.

THE INDUSTRIAL IMPERATIVE

9.3.1. For many years the signal achievement of the UK broadcasting organisations has been their distance from the national political bureaucracy. In the words of the Pilkington Report, the fact that 'the social aspects of broadcasting are, in a sense, extraneous to the general one of the Postmaster General's business contributes essentially to the independence of the broadcasters.' As the social role of information is recognised to be significant, and as new technologies raise basic industrial issues, that favoured independence is undercut.

9.3.2. Wireless telegraphy began as an incidence of invention and technique. The early devices were operated by entrepreneurs and engineers. The first transmissions were celebrated as wonders of scientific achievement. Governments and financiers and industrialists manoeuvered then as now to invest in the new technologies.

9.3.3. In Britain broadcasting started as a private venture of the Marconi Wireless Telegraph Company and its competitors. But the shadow of regulation was discernible as early as 1920 when the Postmaster General accused the manufacturers of 'interfering with important communications' (mainly ship-to-shore radiotelephone). That autumn the government banned Marconi's Chelmsford studios from further transmission. Marconi's response was immediate; there was no point in manufacturing receivers if nothing could be received. The company lobbied the government and, cleverly, the amateur wireless societies and after twelve months the ban was lifted.

9.3.4. The British Broadcasting Company, set up in 1922, had eight directors, each representing a major manufacturer. The system worked well for a few years. But grander social ambitions came into play. In 1927 the company was transformed into a corporation with a royal charter. That elevation marked the beginnings of a golden age of public service broadcasting, which flourished until the 1970s. Its ending may be marked by the international agreement on satellite broadcasting signed in Geneva in 1977, exactly 50 years later. The process of change is slow and the 1977 WARC did not mean the sudden death of public service broadcasting any more than did the 1927 Charter mark the sudden creation of a fully-fledged public service institution. But the concept espoused in 1927 has been strongly challenged, and the challenge echoes the early days with its motifs of private capital investing in competitive technology.

9.3.5. Unlike the company, the corporation was freed from the direct domination of the manufacturers. It could generate (and did, under John Reith) a powerful force as both public patron and public servant. It evolved a whole series of principles of public service broadcasting, covering programme standards and engineering standards. The latter are often forgotten but make a considerable contribution to the overall reputation of the BBC and the IBA.

9.3.6. This tradition was the seed-bed for ITV and Channel Four which, together with BBC-1 and BBC-2, manifest what is correctly called the 'ecology of British broadcasting'. The result is a positive synergy on a scale probably unequalled elsewhere in the world. Government has intervened at certain turning points but in each case has been notable for listening to and agreeing with the constituency of professional broadcasters rather than imposing its own ideas and interests.

9.3.7. This professional independence is now challenged. For many years the UK's broadcasting policy has been merely practical, with little rationale. It was enough to know that it worked. Indeed, the words 'broadcasting policy' were seldom used. The phrase might be said to smack of control and interventionism on too grand a scale. But in March 1982 the Home Secretary used it. He had acknowledged the new industrial context when he had announced the government's decision on satellite broadcasting which, he said, was taken sooner rather than later, and was in favour of an 'early start'. The reason was the government's urgent desire to stimulate industry, to create more jobs and to increase exports. These are traditionally the concerns of the Departments of Industry and of Trade, not the Home Office. But on 4 March it was William Whitelaw who espoused them in the House of Commons. The heart of his announcement was that 'the Government now sees a need for early decisions if the industrial opportunities which DBS offers this country are to be grasped in good time, in a situation in which there will be keen international competition. The government has therefore decided in principle that this country should make an early start with DBS with the aim of having a service in operation by 1986.' Later, he added, 'I hope that we will not lose sight of the central factor, which is that [the satellite] will create opportunities for our industry and jobs.'

9.3.8. The new industrial imperative was spelt out by the Information Technology Advisory Panel in their report, *Cable Systems,* published a fortnight later. In their prefatory letter to the Prime Minister the ITAP said: 'We are convinced that there are powerful economic and industrial arguments for encouraging cable systems in the UK.' Later, the Panel acknowledged that 'We have expressed our view on the implications of such a policy for broadcasting and other activities but in the brief time available to us we have not been able to explore such issues in the depth they require.' The priorities are clear. 'Broadcasting and other issues' are not regarded as essential to the making of policy; however, they should be accounted for.

9.3.9. The priority is industrial expansion, now:

We cannot stress too highly the need for speed. The formulation of broadcasting policy in the past has been a protracted process, with major enquiries extending over three or four years and consultations and discussions then occupying a similar period. This is wholly inadequate for the present situation; a delayed decision is, in this case, the same as a negative decision. There is a very limited time in which industrial capability and market opportunity will exist in the UK. Beyond this time, the chance of creating a strong UK presence in cable systems will have disappeared, and with it some thousands of jobs and prospects of substantial export earnings. If cable systems are to be established, they need to be coming into operation at about the same time as DBS services. We assume that the Government will shortly give approval for a 'modest early start' to DBS, i.e. a two-channel service starting in 1986, and we encourage them to do so. This implies that planning for new cable services should start no later than 1983, and preferably earlier. Finance will only be forthcoming if the future prospects for cable systems are sufficiently certain. We refer again to the General Election that has to be held by May 1984. Unless a positive decision on the future regulatory environment for cable systems is forthcoming well before then, and in practice that means mid-late 1982, there is in our view little prospect of a modern cable industry being established in the UK.

9.3.10. The March 1982 budget continued the trend. Sir Geoffrey Howe, Chancellor, and a few days later, Patrick Jenkin, Secretary of State for Industry, were eager to encourage IT not because they recognised the social significance of information but because they saw the economic benefits of expanding Britain's manufacturing industry. The 100% capital allowance on teletext sets bought by TV companies is to continue a further year till June 1983 (at an estimated cost to the Exchequer of £30 million). The similar allowance on Prestel sets is to continue until 1984. An extra £20 million was allocated to new industrial projects including satellites and cable equipment. The government is aware of the large investments made by US and Japanese companies in English (and Scottish) microelectronics factories, and wishes to encourage further expansion. A week after the budget the Nippon Electric Corporation (NEC) announced a £40 million investment in its factory in Livingston, Scotland. It is these kinds of macro-economic developments that increasingly influence the government's support of new technology, from videotex to high-definition television.

MINISTERIAL RESPONSIBILITIES

9.4.1. The government's responsibilities for information and communications have not been co-ordinated until very recently. Different ministries have taken on different services, more on the basis of technologies than their use. Broadcasting found itself the responsibility of the Postmaster General, film became a matter of the Department of Trade, and telecommunications were regarded as a matter for the Department of Industry.

9.4.2. For many years the responsibilities for broadcasting were held by the Postmaster General as part of his general responsibilities for wireless telegraphy. The PMG was not a Cabinet post and Cabinet matters were dealt with by the Leader of the Council or someone similar. In 1968 the Pilkington Report rejected proposals for change, as already mentioned. But the separation of 'the social aspects of broadcasting' and political regulation could not last. Its success depended upon the broadcasting organisations being technically unadventurous and financially stable, in an unchanging world. The conditions were not fulfilled.

9.4.3. Over the next few years the government made several changes to Whitehall's departmental organisation and to the nationalised industries which affected the policy machinery for communications. In 1969, when the Post Office became a nationalised industry, the post of Postmaster General was abolished and all ministerial responsibilities given to the new Minister of Posts and Telecommunications. Then in February 1974 the Labour government abolished the Ministry of Posts and Telecommunications and broadcasting responsibilities were given to the Home Office, where they have remained. The Annan Committee discussed and rejected the idea of a Ministry of Communications. But it did acknowledge that 'eventually governments will have to face the problem of communications policy'. Eventually?

9.4.4. The Post Office, meanwhile, went through further metamorphoses until under the British Telecommunications Act 1981 a new separate body, British Telecom, was established and given monopoly powers over public telecommunications, with certain specific exceptions. An important aspect of the Act was the innovation of private competition on a limited scale. Either BT or, if agreement cannot be reached, the Secretary of State for Industry, can license private bodies to provide public telecommunications services. Already a consortium of BP, Cable and Wireless and Barclays Merchant Bank have received a licence to operate a wideband telecommunications link between some 20 UK towns. This Mercury network could be a trunk distributor of TV and film.

9.4.5. Responsibility for information technology *in toto* is held by the Department of Industry, which has a Minister of State for Industry and Information Technology (Kenneth Baker MP) and an Information Technology Division with an establishment of 60 people. The Department has a separate Posts and Telecommunications Division with about 40 people, and a separate Space Division with about 20.

9.4.6. Its concern with telecommunications, electronics and aerospace, and its aggressive, populist, championing of information technology, has put the Department of Industry close to the centre of the debate over the future of the 'information society'.

9.4.7. Film is the concern of the Department of Trade, where an Under-Secretary of State (Iain Sproat MP) has responsibility for the relevant Publishing, Tourism and Film department. The assignment is revealing. The problems of the film industry are not those of the consumer (except in the matter of censorship, and the matters raised by the Williams Committee): they concern production (especially pre-production finance) and distribution. The department has three main strands of policy: (1) the support of an indigenous production industry; (2) the collection and application of funds to finance such indigenous production (mainly the British Film Fund, financed by the Eady levy on cinema takings); (3) the protection of the cinema as an economic institution and cultural force. The main policy instruments are levy and quota. The department has a statutory duty to consult with the Cinematograph Films Council over most policy matters; but is not obliged to accept the Council's views.

9.4.8. The main initiative in film policy of the last four years has been the proposal for a British Film Authority. Such an authority was first recommended by a Working Party set up in 1975 by Sir Harold Wilson, Prime Minister. The recommendation was accepted in principle and the Working Party was transmuted into an Interim Action Committee on the Film Industry, with Sir Harold Wilson, now a back-bencher, as chairman, and with additional industry representatives. The Committee published its 'Proposals for the Setting Up of a British Film Authority' in 1978; but the Conservative government that took power in 1979 did not respond favourably. Since then the IAC has published further reports, which have stimulated discussion within the industry but not led to much legislative action. The very latest development within the Department of Trade suggests an amalgamation of the CFC and the IAC. Outside these departmental responsibilities there exist a number of other governmental organisations with various interests in policy. Perhaps the most significant is the Information Technology Unit and Advisory Panel within the Cabinet Office (see 5.4.3. above).

9.4.9. The strongest proposal yet for a restructuring of ministerial responsibilities came in 1980 with the publication of a report, *Information Technology*, by the Advisory Council for Applied Research and Development (ACARD) of the Cabinet Office. The ACARD report was a slim document compared to similar efforts in Japan, France and the USA; but it helped the government (and industry) towards the first, crude recognition of the significance of IT. Amongst its four main recommendations was one that 'responsibility for regulation of communications and broadcasting should be exercised by a single government department' (paragraph 7.11). The government did not accept the recommendation. The reasons were partly political and personal (concerning the current holders of the relevant posts, and the composition of the cabinet) and partly a feeling that a junior minister and a lot of intelligent co-ordination at under-secretary level could prevent the existing system from making too many mistakes. It probably won't be enough, but it must be acknowledged that neither ACARD nor anybody else has produced anything like a clear blueprint for departmental restructuring.

9.4.10. The same point, from a different angle, has been reiterated by the Interim Action Committee on the Film Industry (whose chairman, Sir Harold Wilson, gave broadcasting responsibilities to the Home Office). The IAC argued the case strongly in its first report and, most recently, in its comments to the Home Office on satellite broadcasting: 'This presents a unique and never-to-be repeated opportunity to rationalise the divisive, inefficient and counter-productive fragmentation which until now has characterised governmental responsibilities in the moving picture industries.' In a report to the Secretary of State for Trade on 'Proposals for the Setting Up of a British Film Authority' (January 1978, Cmnd. 7071), Appendix A, the Committee expressed views regarding the way in which the fragmentation of government responsibilities contributed to the weakness of the British film industry, adding that ministerial responsibility for broadcasting television would no doubt be studied when government responsibilities as a whole were being considered. The Committee strongly recommended that one Minister should assume co-ordinating power over satellite broadcasting, cable TV, the film and television industries, video and related media.

9.4.11. The need for urgent action was stressed repeatedly in the ITAP report, *Cable Systems*. 'The overall regulatory structure in which cable systems have at present to operate is inappropriate for their widespread development. It involves two independent Departments, the Home Office and Department of Industry, and British Telecom, all of whom could be concerned in licensing one system. The potential for confusion and lack of co-ordination precludes the speedy decisions that we see as essential. But this issue is not confined to cable – it extends into many aspects of IT. We note that the Government has not taken up the proposal in the ACARD report on IT that the regulatory arrangements for IT should be drawn together in a more coherent fashion. Cable systems exemplify perfectly the inappropriateness of present arrangements. We therefore intend to examine the regulatory structures that impinge upon developments in IT and specifically the relative roles of, and the interaction among, the three bodies mentioned above.'

9.4.12. It is not always properly acknowledged that the idea of government intervention means very different things to the TV and film industries. The broadcasting profession tend to see the IBA and the BBC Board of Governors as essentially restrictive; and the IBA members and BBC Governors, in turn, tend to see the Home Office in the same light. For them, government intervention spells regulation and control (there are exceptions of course, but they remain exceptions). An anniversary article in *The Times* on 24 March 1982 (the Home Office 200 years old that week) epitomised that special characteristic when it said the Home Office was 'a producer's rather than a consumer's department. . . the Home Office's main task is the administration of pain'. The telecommunications industry regards British Telecom (especially after the British Telecommunications Act 1981) in the same way. The complaint is that Whitehall interferes too much.

9.4.13. In contrast, the film industry sees government intervention as a benign influence, usually bringing money, directly or indirectly. The film industry wants more government regulation, not less. Whereas the British broadcasting authorities are seen as agents of regulation, the demand for a British Film Authority is fuelled by expectations of government subsidy and support that will bring more freedom. The government's few film regulations (e.g. quotas) are usually seen as in the industry's own interests; and whereas the ITV levy is seen as a drain on the companies' cash profits, the Eady levy, although an indirect charge on cinemas, is seen as a subsidy for producers and thus, over a period, as an indirect subsidy to the whole system, exhibitors included.

9.4.14. These two conventions, utterly different in their origins, traditions and styles, make an amalgamation of the two industries, in terms of government responsibilities, extremely awkward and prone to misunderstanding. A common ground cannot be found in history, but must come from a common view of the future.

INDEPENDENT ANALYSIS

9.5.1. The third major issue is partner to the first. The information and communications sector in the economy is now so crucial and so influential that it requires continual monitoring and assessment. The cultural, social, economic and other aspects may require equal attention. It is relevant to look at other national sectors that have major political and social importance; from agriculture to urban design. Each has a number of organisations and centres of independent policy analysis.

69

Many are located in universities or centres of further education; some are more independent, and a few are tied to policy work. At the moment, information and communications as a policy matter has no such resource.

9.5.2. There may be a need for an independent, forceful, professional body that could research, criticise and propose ideas and policies on broadcasting and related matters. The body would be permanent, and so accumulate its own wisdom and reputation; and it would have a staff; in these respects alone it would be unlike the Pilkington and Annan commissions of inquiry, or, in their different way, the CFC and IAC.

9.5.3. There have been several models for such a body. One of the first was the old Technical Advisory Committee, which covered all technical matters and provided some useful reports, notably in 1972. The Annan Report recommended a much broader Telecommunications Advisory Committee; but the Labour government in its white paper, *Broadcasting* (1978), said the scope of such a TAC would be too wide and said the Home Office would establish a Broadcasting Technical Advisory Committee; but the Conservative government rejected even that modest proposal.

9.5.4. The various TACs were concerned only with technical matters. There have been several proposals for a rather more substantial body that would engage in the entire range of policy matters. A substantial proposal for a National Broadcasting Centre was submitted to Annan by Anthony Smith, now Director of the BFI, and Jay Blumler, Director of the Centre for Television Studies, Leeds University, under the auspices of the Standing Conference on Broadcasting. The National Broadcasting Centre would be a conglomerate of research, criticism, judgment and publicity. Its basis would be a varied mix of studies; a professional staff would use these studies to monitor and analyse the broadcasting services; it would have a complaints division, and so on. Annan was sceptical, and after discussion remained unconvinced. Perhaps the committee disliked the idea of professional expertise. Anyway, it suggested as its own preference a Public Inquiry Board which would not be so interventionist but would simply channel the public's views. But Annan was half-hearted here as elsewhere and the Labour Government found it easy to reject the proposal for a Public Inquiry Board. It did propose Service Management Boards for the BBC (one for TV, one for radio and one for the External Services) which were to include external appointments; but this blatantly interventionist gesture, which had political origins, fell down at the political hurdles. A rather different Public Enquiry Board was proposed by Lord

Donaldson in the Lords as an amendment to the Broadcasting Bill 1981, but it found little favour and was withdrawn.

Appendix A

1. *Home Office,* 50 Queen Anne's Gate, London SW1 (01-213 3000)
Mr William Whitelaw M P, Secretary of State
Lord Elton, Under Secretary of State
Mr Michael Moriarty, Assistant Under Secretary, Broadcasting Department
Mr Anthony Butler, Assistant Secretary, Broadcasting Department

2. *Department of Trade,* 1 Victoria Street, London SW1 (01-215 7877)
Lord Cockfield, Secretary of State
Mr Iain Sproat M P, Under Secretary of State
Mr D. Eagers, Under Secretary, Competition Policy, Tourism & Other Service
Industries Division
Mr D. Gatland, Assistant Under Secretary, Competition Policy, Tourism &
Other Service Industries Division (and Head, Films Branch)

Cinematograph Films Council
Chairman: Dame Elizabeth Ackroyd
Secretary: Mr David Hill

Interim Action Committee on the Film Industry
Chairman: Sir Harold Wilson M P
Secretary: (vacant)

3. *Department of Industry,* 123 Victoria Street, London SW1 (01-212 7676)
Mr Patrick Jenkin M P, Secretary of State
Mr Kenneth Baker M P, Minister of State for Industry & Information
Technology
Mr John Butcher M P, Parliamentary Under Secretary of State for Industry
Mr Alastair Macdonald, Under Secretary, Head, Information Technology
Division
Mr Andrew Duguid, Head, Policy Unit

4. *Information Technology Unit,* Cabinet Office, 70 Whitehall, London SW1
(01-233 3000)
Mr Brian Unwin
Mr Roger Courtney
Mr Adrian Norman

5. *British Telecom*
Sir George Jefferson, Chairman
Mr Peter Benton, Managing Director, Telecommunications
Mr John Whyte, Deputy Managing Director (Technology)
Mr R. E. J. Back, Senior Director, Networks
Mr John Price (B T representative on Eutelsat, Intelsat)

Appendix B

(a) *A house in London*

An average London household might have one large TV set (now used for much more than TV but the old name lives on) that is capable of receiving Prestel and teletext, and several other smaller sets; perhaps one in the bedroom, one in the kitchen and one integrated with the word-processor. The spare bedroom has an old set which doesn't work very well. The main set has a video cassette player attached; the bedroom set has another cassette player used only for playback. The household subscribes to a cable network and can receive about 30–40 channels of TV. There might be a disc system, and several mini-computers. The amount of redundant equipment and trailing wires would be an acknowledged hazard; only the rich can afford integrated systems. A few people have converted a study, garage, scullery, larder, etc., into information rooms. The total cost of information gathering, processing and display is high; the household's largest single expenditure after dwelling, food and transport. In 1982 prices the TV licence costs £46; the cable subscription costs £120 for the basic service and £50 for the satellite services; cable security costs another £50 (but the insurance company gives a discount of 20% to all people who have interactive security systems); the computer software costs £20; Prestel costs about £50 and the expenditure on pre-recorded cassettes (and possibly discs) is as much as £250. The total annual running costs are about £600. Annual expenditures on equipment, etc. are about £300. A grand total of £1,000.

(b) *A farm in Norfolk*

Isolated villages are often unprofitable customers for both private cable systems and the competitive-minded British Telecom, so most country people cannot benefit from the cable 'revolution'. The local cinemas have closed, too, although there have been several experiments with video projection. But the need for home entertainment, especially during the winter, is higher than ever, so a typical country household would spend heavily on pre-recorded cassettes and discs, and the richer ones would have a personal satellite dish. In the South an ordinary dish might pick up about 15 different satellite programmes (of which seven are English language) while in the North it might pick up seven programmes (five English). In addition to the ordinary domestic services many farmers subscribe to an agricultural information service delivered by satellite and videotex (based on the US Green Thumb service that started way back in the 1970s). The household's domestic bill is about £350; the professional bill is about £2,000 (tax free).

(c) *An office in Birmingham*

An office in the 1990s will be not so much a place for people to gather but a crossroads of information. In 1990 the numbers of people working in Information Technology will be much higher than in 1980, but as productivity increases the figures will probably drop below the 1980 level. Everyone will have a video terminal as he/she now has a telephone; the terminal will function as a computerised telephone/facsimile/telex/teletex/videotex terminal. Most businesses will calculate an employee's information and communication costs as equivalent to their salary/PAYE costs. In spite of the ease with which people can work at home, most people will feel reluctant to do so.